SOFT TOYS
TO SEW

SOFT TOYS
TO SEW

SHEILA M^cGRAW

A FIREFLY BOOK

To Mary Baughen, who gave
so freely of her time, good
humor, energy and
inspiration to this project.

Edited by Sarah Swartz
Photography by Joy von Tiedemann
Design, diagrams, cartoons and patterns by Sheila McGraw

Canadian Cataloguing in Publication Data

McGraw, Sheila
Soft toys to sew

ISBN 1-895565-11-1

1. Soft toy making.   I. Title.
TT174.3.M34 1992   745.592'4   C92-094737-9

A FIREFLY BOOK

Published by:

Firefly Books Ltd.
250 Sparks Avenue
Willowdale, Ontario, Canada
M2H 2S4

Published in the U.S. by:

Firefly Books (U.S.) Inc.
P.O. Box 1325
Ellicott Station,
Buffalo, NY
14205

Printed and bound in Canada

Contents

Getting Started

R ecently, I glanced into a car window at a boy of about nine years of age. He was plugged into his walkman, hand-jiving and lip synching to rap, with his baseball cap pulled way down to his mirrored glasses and the collar of his black jacket flipped up over his ears. This was one cool dude. And there on his lap was his well-worn stuffed doggy.

Girls have always been encouraged to enjoy the company of their dolls.

Children of all ages need the comfort of an enduring and ever present love-object. Psychologists and educators tell us that children need to nurture as well as to be nurtured. Encouraging tenderness and affection in a child is now recognized as a prerequisite to bringing up healthy, independent, well-adjusted adults. In other words, everyone needs to act out their tender side; everyone needs their hugs. And everyone loves to hug a soft toy.

Somber colored toys have evolved into the bright and cheerful characters of today.

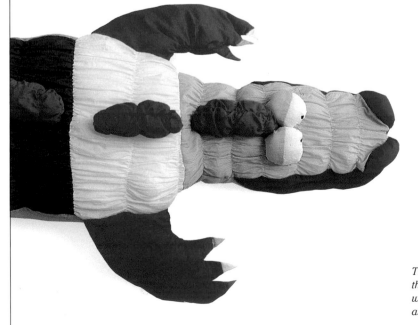

The county fair holds the perennial hope of winning a toy as big as you are.

Historically, early stuffed toys defied the label soft, because most were filled with horse hair, straw or wood chips. Nonetheless, these toys with their naive proportions, crude finishing and hard stuffing were well loved and display the wear and tear to prove it, with their missing eyes, worn fur and bald patches. These old toys — symbols of childhood innocence and comfort — are now prized by collectors and fetch staggering prices at auctions and in antique stores. Today, many classics are manufactured as collectible reproductions.

This stuffed pull-toy , dating from the turn of the century, was found under an attic floorboard of a house undergoing renovation.

Early commercially made bears and other animals dating from the mid 1800s often had jointed legs, arms and heads. Some were mechanical or clockwork; others rode on wooden wheels. While many stuffed animals were mass produced, a large number were handmade at home from scraps of cloth left over from other sewing projects.

Today, technological advances in pile fabrics and synthetic filling have afforded the home sewing enthusiast the opportunity to make professional looking, hygienic, expertly crafted and, most importantly, safe toys.

The advent of the soft toy allowed boys a love-object parallel to girls' dolls.

Working With Plush

Soft toy makers, rejoice. Technology has given us an incredible choice of both realistic and expressive designs, colors and textures in pile fabrics that are springy, dense and supple. When choosing plush, go by the feel of the pile and the suppleness of the backing. Coarse pile and stiff backing say bathmat or toilet seat cover, not Teddy bear. And since Teddy or Monster or Pussycat require such tiny yardage, costs will be low. Buy the best. The best has fine, soft resilient pile and lots of it. The backing should be a soft knit and should not be visible through the pile. With top quality plush, even folding the pile sharply will not expose the backing.

PATTERN LAYOUT

You may wish to pre-wash the plush before cutting. (See "Care", page 15.) Each project has a cutting layout. Follow it closely. All pattern pieces for plush creatures are cut one at a time. This is because plush is bulky and whether you cut with scissors or a cutting wheel, doubling the plush will make the cutting inaccurate. Lay the plush pile-side-down, placing the pattern pieces on the wrong side. You can pin the pattern pieces in place or trace around them with a marker.

Nap

Most pile fabrics have a nap. This is not the sleepy type of nap, of course. Nap occurs when pile on fabrics, such as plush, velvet and some woolens, consistently angles in one direction. The nap runs in line with the selvedge edge of the fabric. Usually you can determine the direction of the nap by running your hand over the fabric in line with the selvedge. The direction of the nap is the direction with the *least resistance*. Often the nap will be visible by turning the fabric, with the color of the pile becoming darker as you look into the nap and lighter as you look along the nap.

Not all plush fabrics have nap. Some that are similar to sheared beaver or lambswool are napless, as are those with a very short fuzzy finish.

All pattern pieces for plush beasties are marked with nap arrows. Be certain these arrows run in the same direction as the nap.

Pinning

Like finding half the worm in an apple, finding a pin the nasty way in a cuddly stuffed animal is painful for the child and embarrassing for the toymaker. To avoid unpleasant surprises, use pins only on the wrong side of the plush and use bead-headed pins which are far more visible and easier to retrieve than regular steel straight pins.

If you must use pins on the right side of the plush to position a head, nose or other part, use bead-headed or extremely large upholstery pins. *Never use regular straight pins on the pile side.* They disappear into the fur and occasionally the heads will pull through to the wrong side, making them very difficult to retrieve. Always count how many pins are used, write the number down and do a tally at the end.

Losing a pin in plush will result in a soft toy that "bites" its owner.

Marking

The dense pile and heavy backing of plush allows you to draw the pattern, notches and other markings onto the wrong side of the fabric with marker. This saves time and constant referrals back to the pattern pieces. Marking the notches inside the cutting line makes for speedy cutting. You can whiz right past, instead of tediously cutting around them. Dots, nap direction and other pattern information are easy to find when you need them. You can even label the pieces with their section names.

Test the marker on the wrong side of a scrap of plush to be sure it won't show through. Some markers are extra juicy and they can bleed through the backing and into the pile, especially if the pile is very soft, pale, short or thin.

When tracing around paper pattern pieces, ensure that pattern pieces do not become too enlarged or distorted by cutting your paper pattern on the inside edge of the cutting line. Then trace tightly around it.

CUTTING

As you cut through plush, a lot of fibers are trimmed. This results in short hairs that lie on the cutting table, cling to the plush and float in the air. Very fine fibers that are released can be inhaled, a rather unhealthy prospect.

There is no perfect solution to avoid the mess, but if it's expected, there are some precautions that can be taken. If you suffer from asthma or allergies, a plasterer's mask might be a good idea. Having a dustbuster handy to pick up the bulk of cut

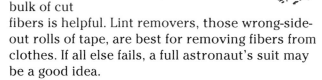

fibers is helpful. Lint removers, those wrong-side-out rolls of tape, are best for removing fibers from clothes. If all else fails, a full astronaut's suit may be a good idea.

Scissors

Scissors are very acceptable cutting tools for plush. The advantage of cutting with scissors is accuracy which always makes for a well made finished product. Choose a good quality pair that are sharp, medium sized and light weight.

Cutting plush with scissors is hard work, especially if the pile and backing is dense and heavy. If you are sewing a large project, you'll need patience in the cutting. The problem with using scissors is that they cut through the pile, not just the backing, releasing those tiny airborne fiber particles. Using scissors can also create a ridge of bristly, short

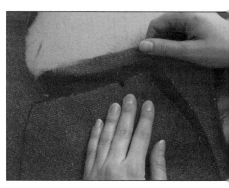

hairs along the seam. When cutting long pile or shag with scissors, try to slide the scissors through the pile so that you are cutting only the backing.

Wheel

If you've been looking for an excuse to purchase a cutting wheel and the necessary cutting board, cutting plush is it. Cutting pile fabrics with this tool is exceptionally fast, easy and less messy. The accompanying cutting board has the added convenience of being gridded, helpful for pattern enlargement.

When cutting plush with the wheel, always cut on the wrong side of the fabric through a single thickness. Cut out the pattern pieces and either pin them in place or trace around them. Cut directly on the line. Most cutting wheels have settings for different fabric weights which makes for less exertion and mess.

Knife

If you become frustrated with scissors, but don't own a cutting wheel, an X-acto knife may be the answer. Although cutting with a knife has drawbacks, there are a few advantages. First the drawbacks: lack of control makes for uneven pressure, slipping and the risk of personal injury. If you press lightly enough to cut only the backing, there are usually many missed threads that will have to be cut with scissors, which is somewhat like doing the job twice. If you press very hard and cut right through, you may slip and cut yourself or cut across the pattern piece.

The advantage of using a knife

comes when cutting shag or long pile, where only the backing of the shag should be cut. If the pile is also cut, you will have lots of short bristly hairs along the seamline. Cut shag by drawing your knife lightly along the cutting line, cutting only the backing. There will probably be many threads of the backing left uncut. These should be clipped with scissors.

Shearing

Shearing pile close to the backing is an effective way to customize a soft toy, giving it a unique and realistic appearance. The ears, muzzles and paws of cats, dogs and Teddies are all enhanced by sheared plush. Check your plush before shearing to determine if the pile near the backing is the same color as the surface pile. Sometimes a two-tone effect is desirable, especially on the face of an animal where the shearing is graduated into longer pile.

It is always best to shear the plush on a cut-out piece which has not yet been sewn. If there is a problem, you won't need to take the

animal apart to fix it. Sometimes shearing before sewing won't work, especially on face or body parts

that need to be sewn together before you can judge how they look. When this happens, proceed slowly and patiently.

To shear plush, lay the section to be trimmed on your hand with the pile up. Trim the pile by laying the scissors flat. First cut it longer than you intend it to be. This can be done quite roughly. Once you have established a general length, trim it smooth to make the pile as even as possible. Often there are hairs that lay down or assume odd angles and they miss being cut. Usually they will pop up on their own over the period of a day or two. They can be trimmed as they appear.

SEWING

Whether your machine is an antique or the latest in electronic wizardry, it doesn't matter when you sew plush. A straight stitch is all you really need. Some of the older machines actually perform better on heavy pile fabrics, because their mechanics are extremely strong and they have better feed and pressure on the presser foot. The only drawback to an older machine is the narrow space under the presser foot. New machines generally have the option to lift the foot higher than normal, which is helpful when inserting bulky pile fabrics.

A myth persists that if you use a large zigzag stitch on plush, the pile will not become caught in the seam. In testing many types and lengths of pile, sewing them with straight and various sizes of zigzag stitches, I have not found this to be the case. A large zigzag stitch is inappropriate for sewing soft toys because of its size and irregularity.

Sewing plush is very satisfying. Plush fabrics don't fray because the backings are knits. This eliminates the need for overcasting and finishing seams. Seams and darts, minor errors and misalignments virtually disappear into the pile.

Seams

Pin all seams well to avoid shifting of the pile during sewing. Use bead-headed pins instead of regular steel ones to prevent losing pins during sewing.

All seams are 1/4 in. (.5 cm) from the raw edge unless otherwise specified. When sewing plush, the silky quality of the pile can cause the layers to slide. Therefore, always baste the seam first with long, straight stitches, (close to the seamline) in the seam allowance. Inspect the seam carefully. The basting allows easy alterations at this point. Then stitch with regular length stitches on the seamline. This will give a reinforced seam that will withstand even the incredible force of a toddler.

When sewing legs, arms or other appendages into a seam, add an extra seam to reinforce these areas. Also reinforce any corners or other stress areas.

Some sewing machines have a triple seam setting. While these seams are very strong, I have found that, in case of an error, they cannot be removed without tearing the fabric. So if you use them, proceed carefully. As stated above, no overcasting or other finishing is required.

Thread

Always use high quality thread for sewing all soft toys. Synthetics like polyester are best as they are very strong, smooth and even. Cotton threads break easily, shrink and often have lumps and other imperfections.

Needles

Needles will often break from sewing plush because of the density of the fabric, especially when there are several layers or seams stacked together. They also break as a result of the bead-headed pins which are bulkier in the fabric than steel pins. Always keep a supply of heavy duty needles on hand. Ball point ones for knits are best although any denim-weight or other heavy needle is fine.

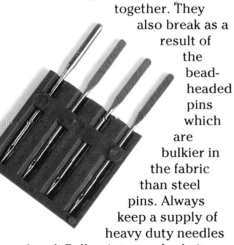

For hand sewing, a long needle, such as a darning needle, is best. Short needles can get lost in the pile. Use the slimmest needle possible. When sewing heavy plush by hand, use a thimble to prevent injury to your needle-pushing finger.

Freeing Pile

Most seams will catch some pile. To free the pile, use a large upholstery pin, a crochet hook or other slim

smooth tool to gently but firmly pull the pile from the seam. Never use the blade of scissors or a knife as it will cut the pile, which will result in short bristly hairs along the seamline, an unattractive prospect. Often with shag or other long pile, catching the pile in the seam can be avoided at the pinning stage by brushing the pile away from the raw edge with your fingers while pinning. This should also be done with any length of pile when the nap of one or both pieces runs toward the seam.

CARE

For hygienic purposes, you may wish to pre-wash your plush before cutting and sewing. Most plush machine-washes and dries very well and pre-washing can improve the texture of the pile and the suppleness of the backing by removing sizing and loose fibres. Before washing the full piece, do a test. Cut a three inch (7.5 cm) square and machine wash it in cold water with a mild detergent. Dry it in the dryer on a low or delicate setting for a short time. Plush dries quickly. Measure for shrinkage.

If machine washing is not acceptable, try another test by hand-washing and line drying another piece. To wash a finished toy, it is advisable to undo the final hand sewing, unstuff the creature and either handwash and fluff the stuffing, or replace it with new stuffing.

Working With Stretch Velour

Purchase the rich velvety stretch velour from which high quality bathrobes are made. With its dense, soft pile it invites touching. It sews wonderfully with nearly invisible seams and it comes in rich jewel tones, pastels and neutrals.

Stretch velour is widely available and is ideal for making small soft toys because the stretch enables tiny or narrow pieces to be turned right-side-out. It is also a knit which means that raw edges will not fray, eliminating the need for overcasting and finishing seams.

While stretch velour will withstand a great deal of wear and tear, it can be damaged by sharp objects which may break a thread and start a hole or a run.

PATTERN LAYOUT

Pre-wash the velour, if desired. (See "Care".) Each project has a cutting layout. Follow it carefully, checking that stretch and nap arrows are in proper alignment. Velour, unlike plush, can be laid out and cut in two or more thicknesses. For multiple thicknesses, lay the fabric right sides together.

Nap

Some stretch velour has a nap. To test for nap, run your hand in line with the selvedge. The direction with the least resistance is the direction of the nap. On most velours the nap is nonexistent or at best inconsequential. However ignoring nap can result in an animal that appears two-toned.

All pattern pieces for velour beasts have nap arrows on them. When laying out your pattern, always have the nap arrows running in the direction of the nap.

Stretch

Stretch velour is a knit and the stretch of any knit runs from selvedge to selvedge. Velour has a particularly strong stretch with good memory so it snaps back time and again, which is excellent for making small soft toys because it enables them to be turned right-side-out easily. Double check that the stretch arrows on the pattern pieces are in line with the stretch of the fabric. Otherwise, small pieces will not turn right-side-out.

Marking

Mark fabric pieces on the wrong side, using tailor's tacks, chalk or pins. Cut all notches outward. If notches are cut inward, they may show as holes along the seam because the seam allowance is quite narrow.

CUTTING

Stretch velour is a beautiful material to handle at every stage and the cutting is no exception. In general, this is an easy to cut fabric and the only drawbacks are a certain amount of mess from cutting through the pile and the tendency of the edges of the fabric to curl. So pin the pattern well.

Scissors

Use very sharp, good quality scissors to cut

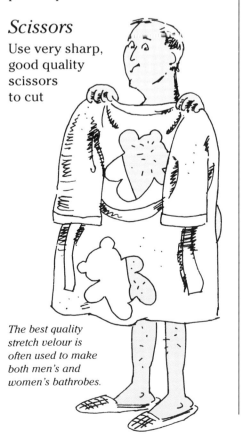

The best quality stretch velour is often used to make both men's and women's bathrobes.

stretch velour. Inexpensive scissors or scissors that aren't properly aligned will bind on this fabric. More than one thickness can easily be cut with scissors, making the process quick and easy. When cutting with scissors, always cut notches outward.

Wheel

A cutting wheel is ideal for cutting velour. Most cutting wheels have a lever to dial the density of the

fabric. This cuts down on the exertion required for cutting lighter weights of fabric such as velour. The accompanying cutting board has the added convenience of being gridded for easier pattern enlargement.

When cutting with the wheel, cut out the paper pattern pieces first and pin them well onto the fabric. Cut directly on the cutting line for greatest accuracy.

SEWING

Pin the velour well, as the raw edges will tend to curl and the pile can cause shifting as you sew. Use bead-headed pins for easy visibility and retrieval. Regular steel pins can pull through the fabric and end up inside your toy. Discard any pins that are rough or catch at the tip, since they might break a thread in the velour, resulting in a hole.

Use matching thread and always sew a double seam on stretch velour. The first seam should be basted using long stitches, close to the seamline in the seam allowance. Check this seam thoroughly, since this is the time to undo and correct any problems. Then sew the second seam with regular-sized stitches on the seamline. This will reinforce the seam. While one seam can be broken by stretching, two seams side-by-side allow the fabric to stretch without problems.

Needles and Thread

Use medium weight ball point needles that are smooth and in good condition. Ball point needles are made for sewing knits. The thread you use should match the color of the fabric, since seams may show. Always use good quality, synthetic thread. It is strong and won't shrink.

CARE

Stretch velour is not only wonderful to look at and to touch, it can be washed and dried by machine many times and it comes back looking great. Choose good quality, soft, synthetic stuffing for the best care results.

Working With Stretch Fleece

While any stretch, knit or good quality fleece with a soft finish is acceptable for making many soft toys, there is one that outshines all the rest. This fleece is called Arctic fleece and it is relatively new. Arctic fleece is a chunky knit that cuts and sews wonderfully. Because it's a knit, the edges of seams never need finishing. It has both fantastic stretch and memory so it snaps back and holds its shape well. Arctic fleece is twice as thick as sweatshirt fleece with fuzz on both sides and it comes in a great range of bright and rich colors.

If you cannot find Arctic Fleece, choose good quality t-shirting, stretch velour, sweatshirt fleece or another stretch fabric.

PATTERN LAYOUT

With no nap and both sides equally right, Arctic fleece is a breeze for pattern layout. The "Cutting Layout" with each project is set up for any type of stretch fleece, whatever its properties. Follow it closely, whichever type of fleece you are cutting.

Nap

In general, most fleece does not have a nap and if it does, it is insignificant on very small pattern pieces. Larger pieces are marked with nap arrows. Place these arrows in the direction of the nap. Test for nap by running your hand parallel to the selvedge. The direction of the nap is the direction with the least resistance.

Stretch

Always buy stretch fleece. If you use woven fleece, small pieces will be impossible to turn right-side-out

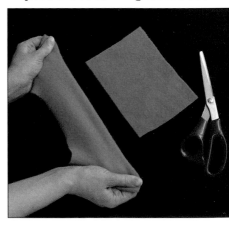

after sewing. Stretch always runs from selvedge to selvedge. Test your fabric for stretch. Then lay pattern pieces with the stretch arrows in the direction of the stretch.

CUTTING

Cutting fleece is easy and straight forward. More than one layer can be cut at a time. The substantial weight of this fabric and the clingy nature of the surfaces means that it won't slip while you are cutting and the cutting is crisp and accurate. Stretch fleece is a knit and has the benefit of never fraying; therefore seams do not need finishing. Cut all notches outward, as cutting the notches inward can result in holes and runs in the seamline.

Scissors

Scissors are an excellent cutting tool for fleece. Use sharp, lightweight scissors to prevent binding of the fabric and to make the cutting easier and less tiring.

Wheel

A cutting wheel is efficient, fast and easy to use on fleece, especially if it can be adjusted to suit the weight of the fabric. Pin cut-out pattern pieces onto the fabric according to the cutting layout and cut directly on the cutting line.

SEWING

Every stage of working with fleece is a pleasure and the sewing is no exception. Fleece doesn't bind, slip or shift in the sewing. It is not overly bulky and the stitches barely show. Because of the stretch, it is often not necessary to notch or clip curves.

Seams

Always pin well with bead-headed pins to prevent the fabric from shifting while sewing. Baste seams first with long machine stitches close to the seamline, in the seam allowance. Check the seam carefully making any corrections. Then stitch a final seam on the seamline. This will create a reinforced seam which will also have some stretch.

Needles and Thread

Use medium weight ball point needles for machine sewing. These needles are made for sewing knits. Thread should match the color of the fabric, since seams may show. Use only high quality, synthetic thread, as it is strong and won't shrink.

CARE

Machine wash and dry.

Working With Textured Nylon

Be careful not to get the wrong type of nylon. Textured nylon is light-weight, similar to a silk weight. It has a subtle irregular texture and it doesn't fray. Other nylons with different weaves are very smooth and shiny and tend to fray like crazy. Textured nylon is available in a large range of interesting colors. Choose from neons, neutrals and rich brights.

If you wish to substitute another woven for this type of nylon, test it for fraying first. If it does fray, you may need to overcast the raw edges before you sew.

PATTERN LAYOUT

Pattern layout is a snap with textured nylon, because it has no nap, no stretch, no grain and no right or wrong side. However, pay attention to the "Cutting Layout," matching grainlines and any other pertinent arrows, if you have substituted a fabric with grain.

Grain

The grain of a fabric follows the direction of its woven threads. If you have chosen a fabric with an obvious cross weave, place the grainline arrows on the grain of your fabric.

CUTTING

Good quality, sharp scissors are excellent for cutting textured nylon. A cutting wheel can also be used, especially if it has a setting for lightweight fabrics. Textured nylon or similar fabrics are generally light

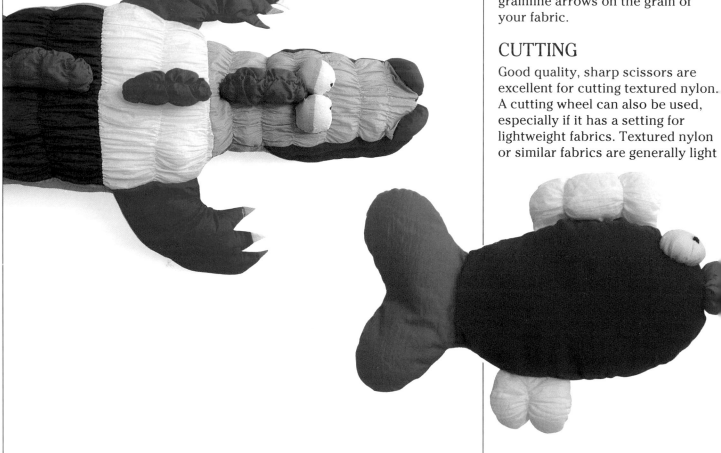

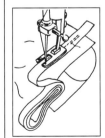

and slippery and patterns need to be pinned very well. They also benefit from being weighted down by a heavy book or another heavy object.

SEWING

The slippery quality of textured nylon makes it necessary to pin it well. Using matching thread, baste all sections with long stitches, close to the seamline inside the seam allowance, before sewing on the seamline. This fabric looks and feels best if it is gathered along seams, either by drawing up basting stitches or sewing seams with elastic. Gathered seams make a creature more appealing, plump and scrunchy. The raw edges of textured nylon will not fray. However, if you have chosen another fabric that does fray, sew the raw edges with an overcast or zigzag stitch.

Sewing Elastic

Use narrow flat elastic and sew it into a seam or onto a single thickness of fabric as follows. Do not cut the elastic into lengths before sewing. Rather, let it come from its skein as needed.

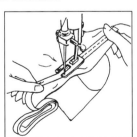

1 Start by allowing the elastic to lie beyond the starting point or edge of the fabric, where it can be grasped. This

will help prevent the elastic from being pulled down into the needle hole. Anchor with three or four stitches. Do not stretch the elastic yet.

2 Without stretching the elastic, sew to the seamline. Now that the elastic is well anchored, stretch the elastic as tightly as possible. Apply equal pressure to the elastic in front of, and behind, the needle. Using either a zigzag or a straight stitch and regular sized stitches, sew the length of the seam, easing pressure on the elastic only near the end.

Note: If using a zigzag stitch, be sure that the needle pierces the elastic regularly, instead of creating a channel in which the elastic can move freely.

3 Cut the elastic.

CARE

Machine wash and dry or line dry. Nylon dries very quickly.

Eyes

The eyes have it. No matter how finished your creature is, no matter how much personality it has, no matter how beautiful the fabrics and colors are, it only comes to life when the eyes are on. There are several types of eyes that can be purchased in craft stores, sewing supply stores and some fabric outlets.

Children are always attracted to the twinkle in a stuffed animal's eyes and many kids make it their ambition to remove them . . . and swallow them. Therefore, it is important to consider safety first when choosing eyes. Read carefully about the type of eyes you may wish to attach and the safety considerations for each.

Avoid any eyes that are glued on, as well as carny eyes — the flat ones that are sewn on and have a clear front and a loose flat eyeball between the layers. If you use buttons as eyes, always choose them with caution and attach them very securely.

FRENCH KNOTS

French knots are made from a very simple embroidery stitch. They are excellent as eyes for small toys, especially those made from velour or light weight fabrics that cannot accommodate heavy buttons or commercial plastic eyes. A single small dot for each eye can be very expressive, as long as they are not buried in pile. French knots are made with embroidery thread, allowing great choice of color.

X-RAY

Making French Knots

1 From a length of six-strand embroidery thread, separate three strands. Thread needle and knot end. Enter the needle through an inconspicuous seam, exiting the needle where you wish the French knot to be.

2 Wind the embroidery thread around the needle three to five times.

3 Holding the wound thread close to the fabric, enter the needle at the base of the knot, exiting at the spot where you wish to make the next knot, or tie off.

VELCRO DOTS

At the fabric store, you will find packages of Velcro dots in a variety of colors and sizes. These are ideal for smaller projects for which you may wish to have a larger dot than a French knot, but for which the fabric of the soft toy is too light or soft to accommodate larger, heavier commercial eyes.

There are two sides to the Velcro dots. One side is soft and nappy and the other side is burr-like. Only use the soft side of the dots for the eyes.

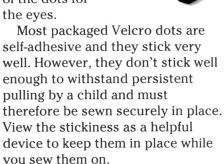

Most packaged Velcro dots are self-adhesive and they stick very well. However, they don't stick well enough to withstand persistent pulling by a child and must therefore be sewn securely in place. View the stickiness as a helpful device to keep them in place while you sew them on.

The only drawback with these dots is the gummy residue that coats the needle as you sew by machine or by hand. To alleviate this problem, try soaping the needle, or purchase Velcro by the yard, which is not self-adhesive and cut circles with scissors.

BUTTONS

I hesitate to suggest the use of buttons, because if they are not fastened securely, they can be chewed off and swallowed by a small child. However, there are ways to attach them that are very strong. And when other types of eyes are not available, buttons make a very worthwhile substitute.

Buttons are generally removed by kids who chew through exposed thread. Therefore, any buttons that show thread, such as two or four-hole flat buttons, are vulnerable and not recommended for use on soft toys.

Attaching Button Eyes

Find two buttons with shanks that are either built-in or very flat, so that the buttons will be very tight to the head of the toy. You will also need two two-hole, flat buttons, larger than the shank buttons. Use only heavyweight thread.

1 Thread the needle, doubled. Check the pattern for placement. Position one shank button on the right side of the fabric and a flat button on the wrong side. Stitch three times.

 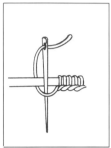

2 Without tying off, position the second eye and another flat button. With the thread bridging the two eyes, sew the second eye in position with three stitches.

3 Without tying off, draw the thread back and forth between the eyes, as you sew them.

4 Reinforce the thread between the eyes with a blanket stitch. Tie off.

COMMERCIAL EYES

At craft stores, sewing supply stores and some fabric stores, you can find the good quality solid plastic eyes used by the top soft toy producers. Use commercial eyes only on plush or very stable fabrics. The hole needed to insert the eye can expand or tear and the eye can easily come out of lightweight wovens and knits. Commercial eyes are available in a multitude of sizes and colors. These eyes have a strong straight plastic

post on the back, which is sometimes ridged, and a circular metal or plastic grommet with a star-shaped hole punched through the center. Once these two components are joined, they will not come apart. Unless your child is adept with power tools, those eyes will stay where you put them. Be absolutely certain the eyes are in the right spot. Once attached, you won't be able to remove them.

Attaching Commercial Eyes

1 Position the eyes according to the pattern. Using a seam ripper, break only one thread on

 the backing of the plush in the center of the eye. Push the post of the eye through.

2 If you are using cats'

eyes (in which pupils are elongated rather than round), check that the pupils run vertically. Place the eye down on a hard surface. Push the metal grommet onto the shank as far as it will go. If the grommet is on properly, there should be no space between the eye and the fabric. Repeat with the remaining eye.

PUFFY FABRIC EYES

Puffy eyes are great on creatures that need a monster or froggy look. These eyes tend to look sleepy, worried or endearingly resigned. They are easy to make and perfectly safe for any child. Because kids like to lug animals around by these puffy eyes, attach them well with a ladder stitch. To make puffy eyes, consult the patterns and sewing instructions for Monster, Crocodile or Frog in the Easy Creatures project. (See pages 76, 152 or 28.) Make dots on center of puffy eyes with satin stitch.

Noses

Most creatures don't need noses. In general they are not a very important part of the face of a soft toy, just as mouths and occasionally ears can be overlooked. If you prefer realism, however, you may want your animal to have a nose.

FABRIC NOSES

If you wish to make a fabric nose, consult the pattern and instructions for Lazy Dog or Party Animal. (See pages 112 or 48.) Lazy Dog's nose is a very pleasing rounded, triangle shape that also suits a Teddy bear. Party Animal's nose is a small triangle that would suit a bunny or mouse equally well. Make fabric noses from stretch velour or another soft knit, so that they are as cuddly as the soft toy to which they are sewn.

SATIN STITCH

Satin stitch is a simple embroidery stitch. If done evenly, the results are a glossy, smooth, professional look.

Use either six-strand embroidery thread or embroidery wool and a large needle.

1 If there is plush at the site of the nose, use small scissors, such as nail scissors, and cut away as much pile as possible in the exact shape of the nose.

2 Thread needle with three strands of six-strand embroidery thread and knot the end. Enter needle through an inconspicuous seam, burying the knot and bringing the needle out at

the top corner of the nose. Continue as shown, by making stitches longer or shorter to fit the width and keeping the pressure even. Exit and tie off through a seam.

COMMERCIAL NOSES

Commercial noses are the molded plastic variety that are realistic looking, but often look out of context because they seem so hard on a soft toy. Those noses usually resemble either dogs' or monkeys' noses and are available in various sizes at craft stores and sewing supply stores. Attach commercial noses in the same way that you apply commercial eyes.

Observing the wear patterns on old toys can help soft toy makers avoid problems on new ones.

Fillings

Early soft toys were not soft. They were packed tightly with straw, horse hair, rags, feathers, wood chips or sand. Today, for sanitary as well as tactile reasons, soft toys are always stuffed with new, clean synthetic fiber. While the synthetic fiber industry produces many different qualities of this white cloud-like material, generally you will find only one low quality available in fabric stores, sewing supply stores and craft stores. Some stores may special-order superior fillings and some better qualities are available by mail order through craft magazines.

QUALITY

Most stores carry one-pound bags of Fiberfil. This is a polyester product and it has the least number of air channels in the fibers, causing it to be dense, non-springy and heavy. It also doesn't have slickener, a silicone-like product that coats the fibers. Fiberfil tends to clump together and become lumpy.

Of far better quality is Hollofil, a product with far more holes in the fibers and a good amount of slickener. Hollofil is light, springy and yielding to the touch. You no doubt have cushions or pillows that have labels reading Hollofil. Best of all is Qualofil, light as a cloud, extremely resilient and long-lasting. This is the filling that makes a soft toy huggable, touchable. The best quality comforters and pillows are made with Qualofil filling.

EXPENSE

When I ask fabric and craft store owners and managers why they won't stock the superior fillings, they always say that it's because of the cost. The irony of this argument is that you only need half as much of the better quality filling. If it takes one pound (500 grams) of Fiberfil to fill the Buzzard, one-half pound (250 grams) of Qualofil will do the same job. This is because of the air in the product and its memory — its ability to return to the same volume. Because low quality fillings have little resilience, you must pack the soft toy very tightly with the filling for it to have any shape. High quality fillings don't require this.

Antique toys filled with straw, sand, rags and horse hair.

In the end, the cost is the same. Pay twice as much for excellent quality and use half as much, or pay half as much for poor quality and use twice as much. Get it?

WHERE TO BUY IT

Good question. Although there must be someone packaging and distributing the good stuffing, I never found it in my fabric or craft stores. I finally called Dupont, the company which manufactures Hollofil and Qualofil and they gave me the name of a distributor who sells small quantities to the public. I have also seen mail order ads for good quality fillings in craft magazines.

If you have no luck, you may have a couple of old pillows put away which you don't use. Check the filling on their labels. If they are suitable, machine wash and dry the pillows. They may become a little lumpy. Don't worry. When you remove the stuffing, process it by ripping it apart. It will become resilient again.

STUFFING

In general, always stuff small areas, such as the appendages of your soft toy, tightly. Large areas, such as the body, should be stuffed more loosely. Be certain that all areas are filled. Otherwise, they will "cave in" later and it will be difficult to rectify without taking the toy apart. The handle of a wooden spoon is an ideal tool to force filling into the ends of legs and tails.

CARE

All synthetic fillings can be washed and dried by machine. However, redistribution of filling can be a problem. The combination of the weight when the filling is wet and the regular motions of the washer and dryer can cause shifting and bunching. The best solution is to open the toy, remove the filling and hand wash it or replace it. Hand washing, drying and massaging the dry toy can also alleviate the problem.

CLOSING

Always close your finished soft toy with a ladder stitch. This is a simple hand stitch that is done from the right side and it is virtually invisible.

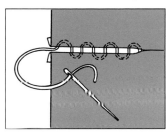

Using doubled thread, knotted, pick up five or six small running stitches in a zigzag fashion on both sides of the seam. Pull tight. Tie off without breaking thread. Repeat to the end of the opening.

Easy Creatures

Variations on one simple pattern make five very different and appealing animals. These cuddly beasts have endearing and enduring qualities. They are small enough for crib toys, yet graphic and colorful enough for older kids. Each has distinctive traits that give it personality and make its species easily identifiable. All are made in the rich jewel tones of soft touchable stretch velour, the perfect foil for a spider's pointy teeth, a crab's menacing pinchers and a turtle's grumpy face.

The dots on the ladybug and the eyes of the spider and crab are the soft halves of Velcro dots which come in various sizes and colors.

Cutting

WHAT YOU NEED

Purchase the best quality stretch velour available. Be sure it has good stretch and soft pile.

ALL ANIMALS

- ¹/₄ yd. (.3 m) velour, 48 in. (120 cm) wide

FROG AND SPIDER

- Scrap, white fabric, 4 in. (10 cm) square

LADYBUG

- Scrap, red fabric, 8 in. (20 cm) square

TURTLE

- Scrap, quilting, 8 in. (20 cm) square

STUFFING

- Two handfuls of synthetic filling

NOTIONS

- *For Frog*: black embroidery thread
- *For Turtle*: matching thread for top stitching
- *For Ladybug*: black Velcro dots

OPTIONAL

- Embroidery thread or Velcro dots for eyes

CUTTING REMARKS

- Position all pattern pieces according to cutting layout. Check whether fabric is single or double thickness and whether patterns are right or wrong side up. (See "Code for Cutting and Sewing".)
- Cut accurately, directly on cutting line.
- Transfer all symbols to wrong side of fabric.
- Cut notches outward.
- Check stretch fabrics. Position stretch arrows in direction of stretch.

FINISHED SIZE

5 in. (13 cm)

CODE FOR CUTTING AND SEWING

Pink denotes RIGHT side of fabric.

White denotes WRONG side of fabric.

Yellow denotes RIGHT side of pattern.

Dots denote WRONG side of pattern.

CUTTING LAYOUT

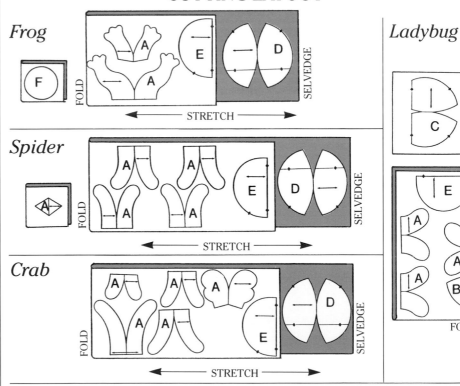

Ladybug

Sewing

KNOW BEFORE YOU SEW

- PINS – Use bead-headed pins for visibility and easy retrieval.
- SEAMS – Make seams 1/4 in. (.5 cm) wide.
- STITCH – Sew medium-length machine stitches.
- BASTE – Sew long machine stitches. Baste all seams before sewing.

Notch curve.   Clip curve.   Clip corner.

- NOTCH CURVE – Cut V's to seam, evenly along curve.
- CLIP CURVE – Clip to seam, evenly along inside curve.
- CLIP CORNER – Clip from inside corner to pivot in seam.
- REINFORCING – Reinforce all stress points with an extra seam.
- STUFFING – Stuff small areas firmly and larger areas less firmly.
- LADDER STITCH – Sew an invisible seam from the right side.

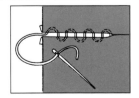

For more information on these, or any other sewing terms consult the glossary at the back of the book.

Appendages for all Creatures

Ladybug: Six Legs.

Crab: Two Claws, Eight Legs.

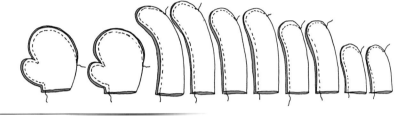

Frog. Four Legs.

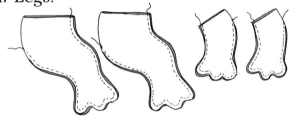

Turtle: Four Legs, One Tail, One Head.

Spider: Eight Legs, Two Teeth.

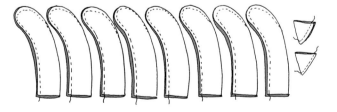

1 All appendage sections are marked (A) on patterns. Make all appendages for your creature — legs, heads, tails, claws or teeth — as follows. Fold one section in half along foldline, as indicated on pattern, with right sides together. Stitch from fold-edge, around curve and to end. Leave end open for turning and stuffing. Repeat for all appendages of your creature.

Notch curves, if necessary. Turn all pieces right-side-out.

2 Stuff all appendages (except spider fangs) firmly. Use the handle of a wooden spoon to insert stuffing if necessary.

Baste open ends shut, close to raw edge.

Turtle only: Match side seams on head section, when basting end shut.

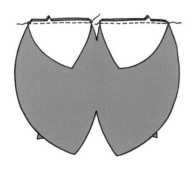

Ladybug only: Position HEAD (B) sections onto BACK (C) section with right sides together, matching notches. Stitch straight, notched edges.

Body for all Creatures

1 Fold BACK (D) section of your creature in half with right sides together. Stitch center seam, including fold-edge.

Optional:

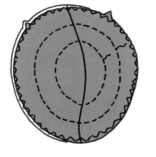

Turtle only: Repeat step 1 using quilt BACK (D) section. Position quilt section onto WRONG SIDE of velour back section. Stitch with a zigzag or straight stitch, close to raw edge. Top stitch two circles.

2 Position two STOMACH (E) sections with right sides together, matching notches. On straight edge, stitch from each notch to end, leaving area between notches open for turning and stuffing.

Crab

Ladybug

Frog

Turtle

Spider

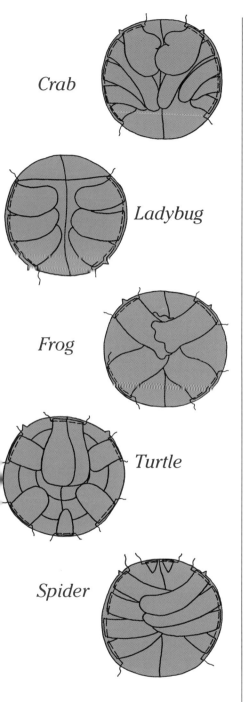

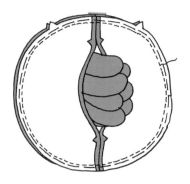

3 Lay back section flat with RIGHT SIDE UP. Position all appendages on RIGHT SIDE of back section. Refer to diagrams above for placement. Baste close to raw edge.

4 Position stomach section onto back section with right sides together, matching notches and seams. To make this easier, push appendages through opening in stomach section. Pin very well. Baste. Check seam. Stitch full outside edge. Turn right-side-out.

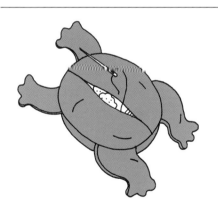

5 Stuff body with filling through opening in stomach. Using good quality thread, doubled, sew opening with ladder stitch.

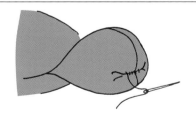

Turtle only: Create tuck in face. Fold along foldline, as indicated on pattern, matching small •s. Slip stitch lips together.

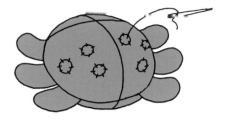

Ladybug only: Create spots by sewing the soft halves of several black Velcro dots onto red back of ladybug.

Frog only: Create froggy eyes. Baste close to raw edge of one EYE (F) section. Gather basting gently and stuff firmly. Then gather very tightly and tie off. Using good quality thread, doubled, stitch eyes in place with ladder stitch.

Satin stitch black dots in center of eyes with heavy black thread or embroidery thread.

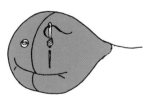

6 Create eyes from Velcro dots or French knots. (See page 22 for more information.)

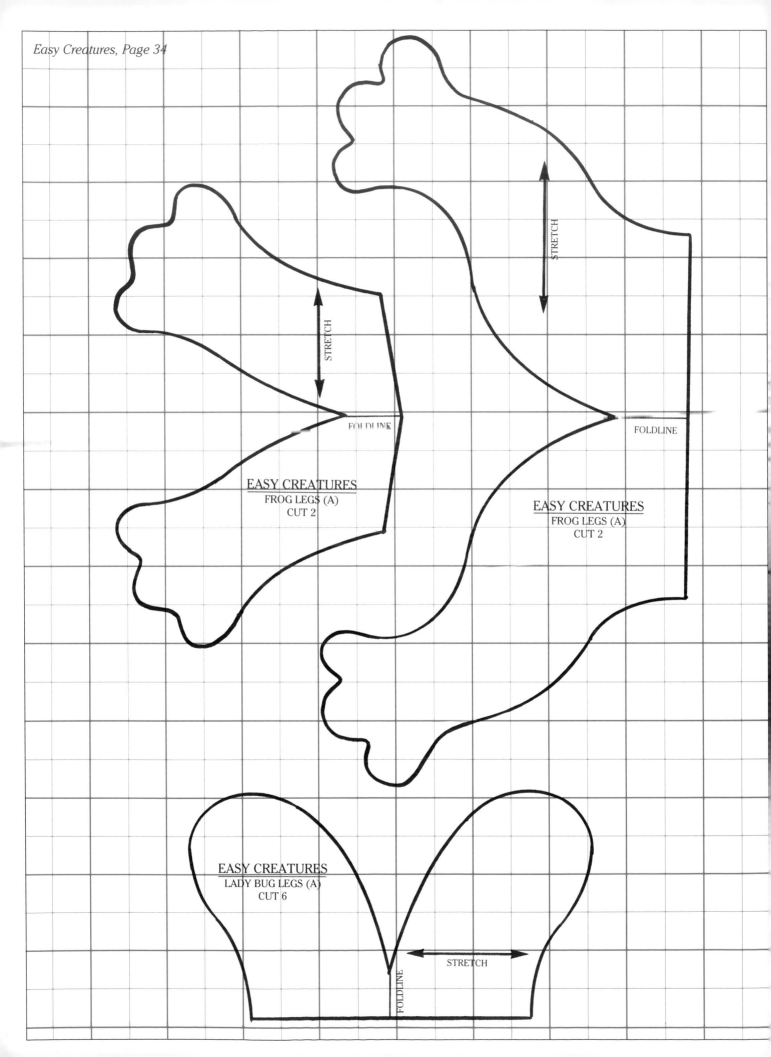

STRETCH

STRETCH

FOLDLINE

FOLDLINE

EASY CREATURES
FROG LEGS (A)
CUT 2

EASY CREATURES
FROG LEGS (A)
CUT 2

EASY CREATURES
LADY BUG LEGS (A)
CUT 6

FOLDLINE

STRETCH

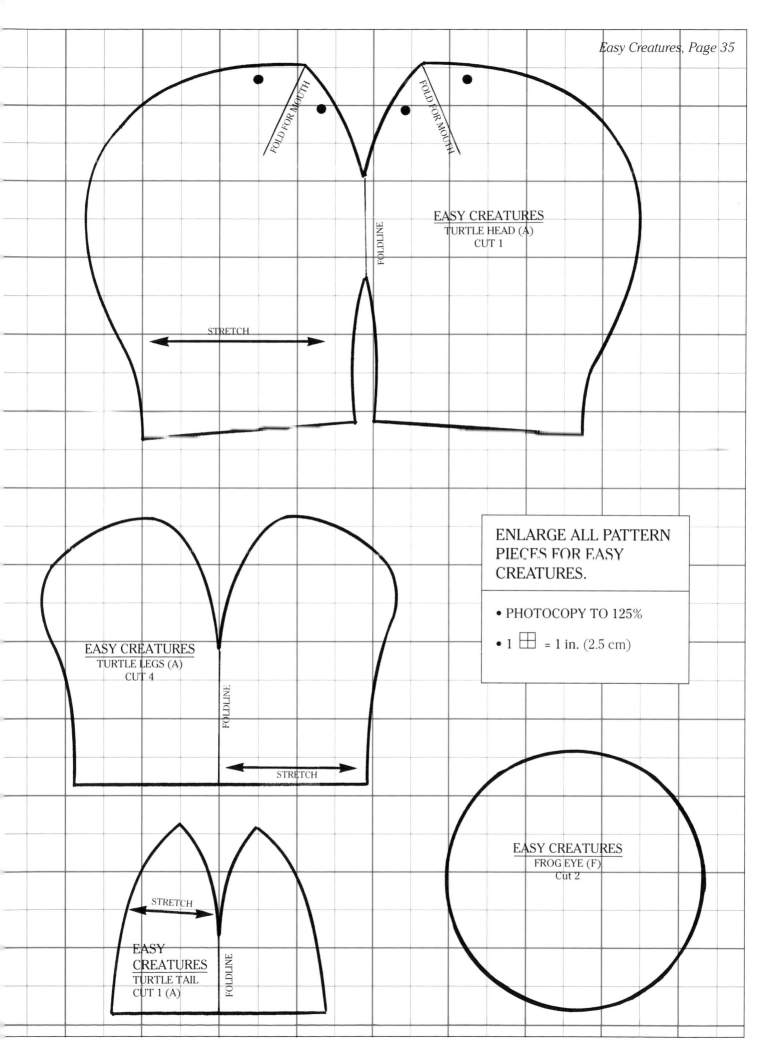

FOLD FOR MOUTH

FOLD FOR MOUTH

EASY CREATURES
TURTLE HEAD (A)
CUT 1

FOLDLINE

STRETCH

EASY CREATURES
TURTLE LEGS (A)
CUT 4

FOLDLINE

STRETCH

ENLARGE ALL PATTERN
PIECES FOR EASY
CREATURES.

• PHOTOCOPY TO 125%

• 1 ⊞ = 1 in. (2.5 cm)

STRETCH

EASY
CREATURES
TURTLE TAIL
CUT 1 (A)

FOLDLINE

EASY CREATURES
FROG EYE (F)
Cut 2

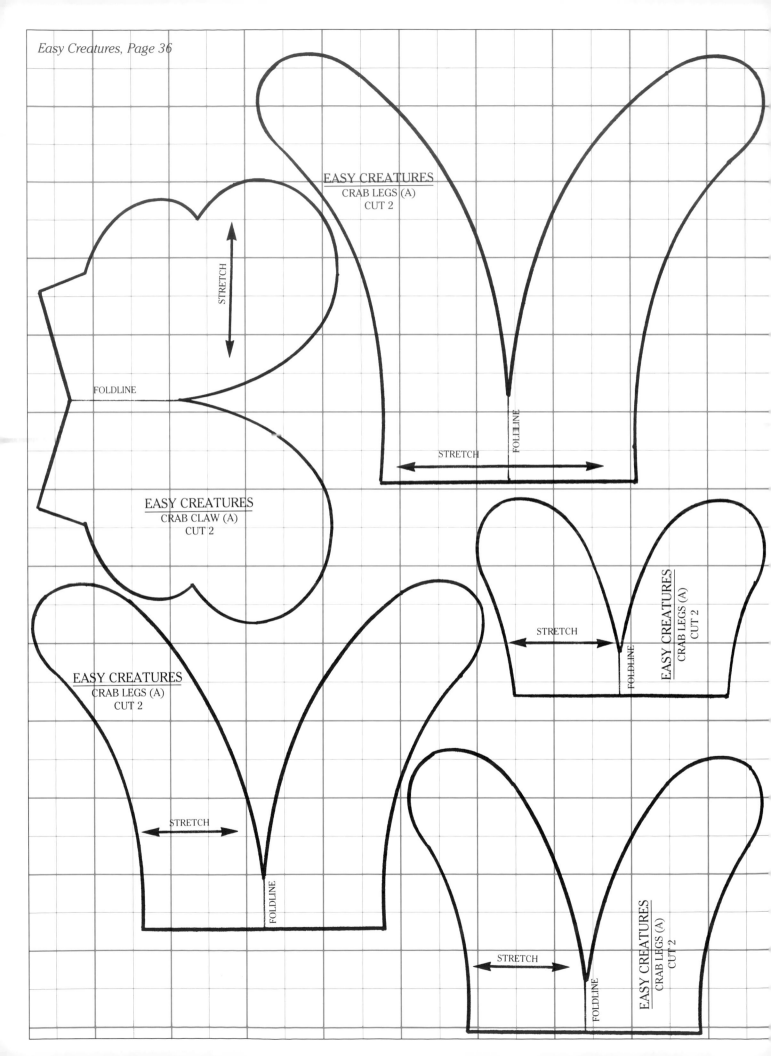

EASY CREATURES
CRAB LEGS (A)
CUT 2

STRETCH

FOLDLINE

STRETCH

EASY CREATURES
CRAB CLAW (A)
CUT 2

FOLDLINE

EASY CREATURES
CRAB LEGS (A)
CUT 2

STRETCH

FOLDLINE

EASY CREATURES
CRAB LEGS (A)
CUT 2

STRETCH

FOLDLINE

EASY CREATURES
CRAB LEGS (A)
CUT 2

STRETCH

FOLDLINE

EASY CREATURES
CRAB LEGS (A)
CUT 2

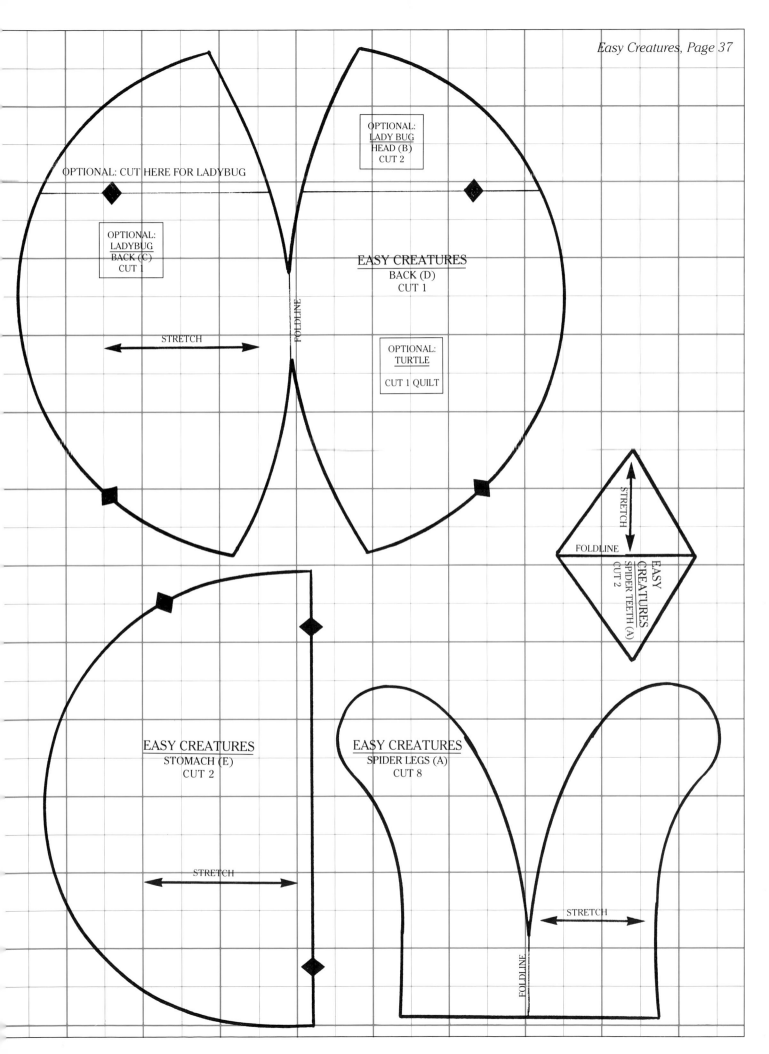

OPTIONAL: CUT HERE FOR LADYBUG

OPTIONAL:
LADY BUG
HEAD (B)
CUT 2

OPTIONAL:
LADYBUG
BACK (C)
CUT 1

EASY CREATURES
BACK (D)
CUT 1

STRETCH

FOLDLINE

OPTIONAL:
TURTLE

CUT 1 QUILT

STRETCH

FOLDLINE

EASY
CREATURES
SPIDER TEETH (A)
CUT 2

EASY CREATURES
STOMACH (E)
CUT 2

EASY CREATURES
SPIDER LEGS (A)
CUT 8

STRETCH

STRETCH

FOLDLINE

Kissy Fishy

C hunky lips, googly eyes, neon brights and an all-over cartoon look combine in an easy project for fin-tastic results. Make just one for hugging or a whole school of squishy, multicolored fishies for a snappy hanging. These colorful fish make great accents in the kitchen or bathroom. Sew them from washable, fast drying, neon textured nylon or any light-weight woven that's crisp and silky. When made with synthetic filling and lightweight terry, this fish can be a child's favorite washcloth. For a decorator touch, go with silk or designer prints.

The construction of this fish is based on gathering seams as you go. The gathers are what gives the fish its shape and scrunchy appeal. (See glossary for more information on gathering.) If you are good at sewing with elastic, you can substitute elastic for the gathers. (See page 21 for more information on sewing with elastic.)

Cutting

WHAT YOU NEED

Purchase crisp-yet-silky wovens that fray very little, such as textured nylon. Various blends, broadcloth or chintz, stretch fabrics like velour, terry, fleece or t-shirting may also be used. Since small quantities are required for this multicolored fish, you may wish to purchase remnants or simply use what is around the house.

KISSY FISHY

- Remnant, 16 in. (45 cm) square for body
- Scrap, 10 in. (25 cm) square for tail
- Scrap, 10 in. (25 cm) square for top fin
- Scrap, 8 in. (20 cm) square for bottom fin
- Scrap, 8 in. (20 cm) square for lips
- Scrap, 8 in. (20 cm) square for eyes

STUFFING

- ¼ lb. (125 g) synthetic filling

NOTIONS

- Matching thread
- Embroidery thread for eye dots

OPTIONAL

- 1½ yd. (1.5 m) narrow, flat elastic

CUTTING REMARKS

- Position all patterns according to cutting layout. Check whether fabric is single or double thickness and whether patterns are right or wrong side up. (See "Code for Cutting and Sewing".)
- Cut accurately, directly on cutting line.
- Transfer all symbols to wrong side of fabric.

FINISHED SIZE

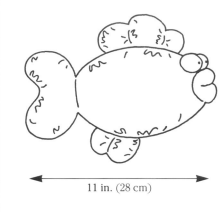

11 in. (28 cm)

CODE FOR CUTTING AND SEWING

Pink denotes RIGHT side of fabric.

White denotes WRONG side of fabric.

Yellow denotes RIGHT side of pattern.

Dots denote WRONG side of pattern.

CUTTING LAYOUT

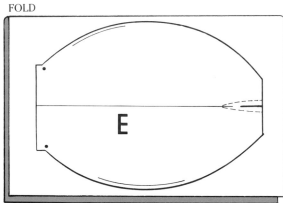

FOLD

E

SELVEDGE

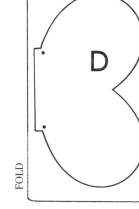

D

FOLD

SELVEDGE

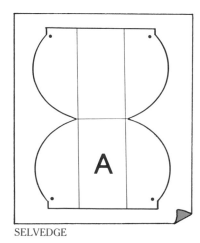

A

SELVEDGE

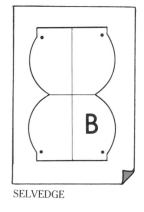

B

SELVEDGE

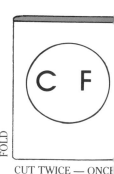

C F

FOLD

CUT TWICE — ONCE LIPS, ONCE FOR EYE

Sewing

KNOW BEFORE YOU SEW

- PINS – Use bead-headed pins for visibility and easy retrieval.
- SEAMS – Make seams 1/4 in. (.5 cm) wide.
- STITCH – Sew medium-length machine stitches.
- BASTE – Sew long machine stitches. Baste all seams before sewing.

Notch curve.　Clip curve.　Clip corner.

- NOTCH CURVE – Cut V's to seam, evenly along curve.
- CLIP CURVE – Clip to seam, evenly along inside curve.
- CLIP CORNER – Clip from inside corner to pivot in seam.
- REINFORCING – Reinforce all stress points with an extra seam.
- STUFFING – Stuff small areas firmly and larger areas less firmly.
- LADDER STITCH – Sew an invisible seam from the right side.

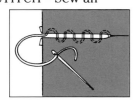

For more information on these or any other sewing terms, consult the glossary at the back of the book.

Fins

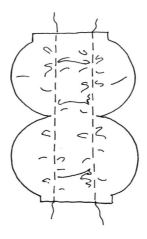

1 On TOP FIN (A) section, baste long stitches on two gather lines, marked on pattern. Use thread to match fabric. Gather by pulling bobbin thread until each seam is approximately 5 in. (12 cm) long.

2 Stay stitch gathers by sewing with small stitches, close to basting stitches.

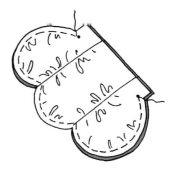

3 Fold fin section in half along foldline, as marked on pattern, with right sides together. Baste between •s, including fold-edge.
　Gather gently, drawing up about one-quarter seam length.

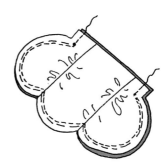

4 Using small stitches, sew full curved edge of fin, close to basting stitches, pivoting at •s. Leave straight edge open for turning and stuffing. Clip corners to •s.

5 Turn fin right-side-out. Stuff gently. Baste open edge shut, close to raw edge. Set aside.

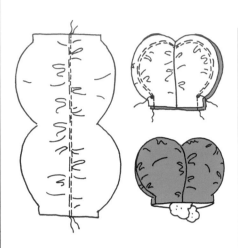

6 Baste BOTTOM FIN (B) along center gather line, as marked on pattern. Gather center to approximately 4 in. (10 cm).

Using small stitches, stay stitch gathering by sewing as close to basting stitches as possible.

Repeat steps 3 through 5 with bottom fin.

Lips

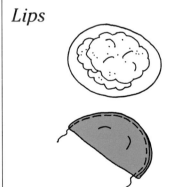

1 Lay one LIPS (C) section flat with WRONG SIDE UP. Place a small wad of stuffing onto lip section.

Fold lip section in half with WRONG SIDES TOGETHER, keeping stuffing inside. Baste curved edge very close to raw edge. Repeat with remaining lips section.

2 Gather basting, until curved edge becomes straight. Repeat with remaining lips section.

Position two lip sections together, matching gathered edge. Tie off gathers. Baste across gathered edge, close to raw edge. Set aside.

Tail

1 Position two TAIL (D) sections with right sides together. Baste curved edge between •s. Gather gently, drawing up approximately one-quarter of seam length.

2 Using small stitches, sew full seam, pivoting at •s. Leave straight edge open for turning and stuffing. Clip corners to •s.

3 Turn tail right-side-out. Stuff with filling. Baste straight edge shut, close to raw edge. Set aside.

Body

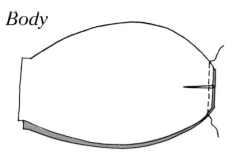

1 Position two BODY (E) sections with right sides together, matching slashes. Stitch short straight nose seam, stitching across slash.

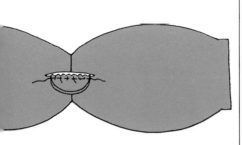

2 Open out body section and lay flat with RIGHT SIDE UP. Lay raw edge of lips against one side of slash. Baste lips in place, close to raw edge.

3 Fold body section in half, LENGTHWISE, with right sides together. Gathered edge of lips should be visible in slash. Pin lips area. Baste tuck in body along slash, as marked on pattern, sewing lips in seam. Stitch.

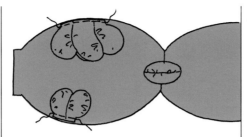

4 Lay body flat with RIGHT SIDE UP. Position top fin and bottom fin onto one body panel. See pattern for placement. Baste in place, close to raw edge.

5 Fold body in half, CROSSWISE, with right sides together. Baste top and bottom curved seams to •s. Gather gently, drawing up approximately one-quarter of seam length.

Using small stitches, sew seams close to gather stitching. Leave straight tail edge open for turning and stuffing. Be sure fins are sewn into seam, but lips are kept free. Clip corners to •s. Turn fish right-side-out.

Finishing

1 Baste very close to raw edge of one EYE (F) section. Gather gently and stuff firmly. Then gather tightly and tie off. Repeat with remaining eye.

2 Using black embroidery or heavy thread, satin stitch a black dot in center of each eye.

3 Using ladder stitch and doubled thread, sew eyes in position. See pattern for placement.

4 Stuff fish with filling through tail opening. Turn in raw edges of tail opening. Position tail in tail opening and top stitch with matching thread.

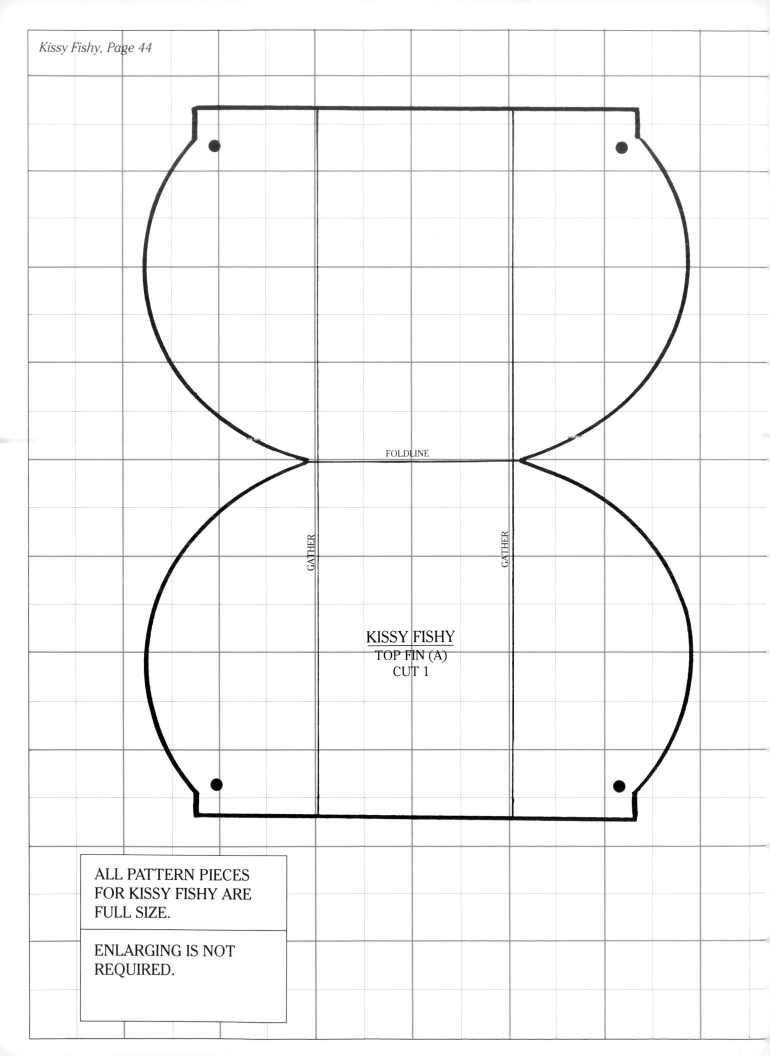

FOLDLINE

GATHER

GATHER

KISSY FISHY
TOP FIN (A)
CUT 1

ALL PATTERN PIECES
FOR KISSY FISHY ARE
FULL SIZE.

ENLARGING IS NOT
REQUIRED.

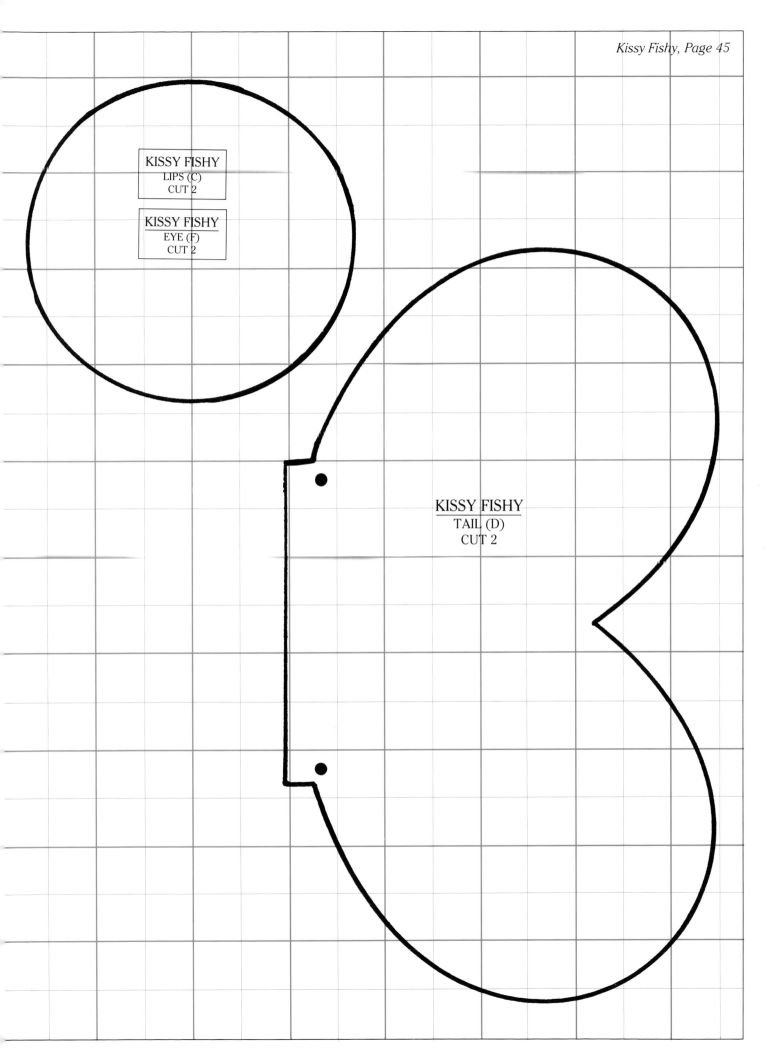

KISSY FISHY
LIPS (C)
CUT 2

KISSY FISHY
EYE (F)
CUT 2

KISSY FISHY
TAIL (D)
CUT 2

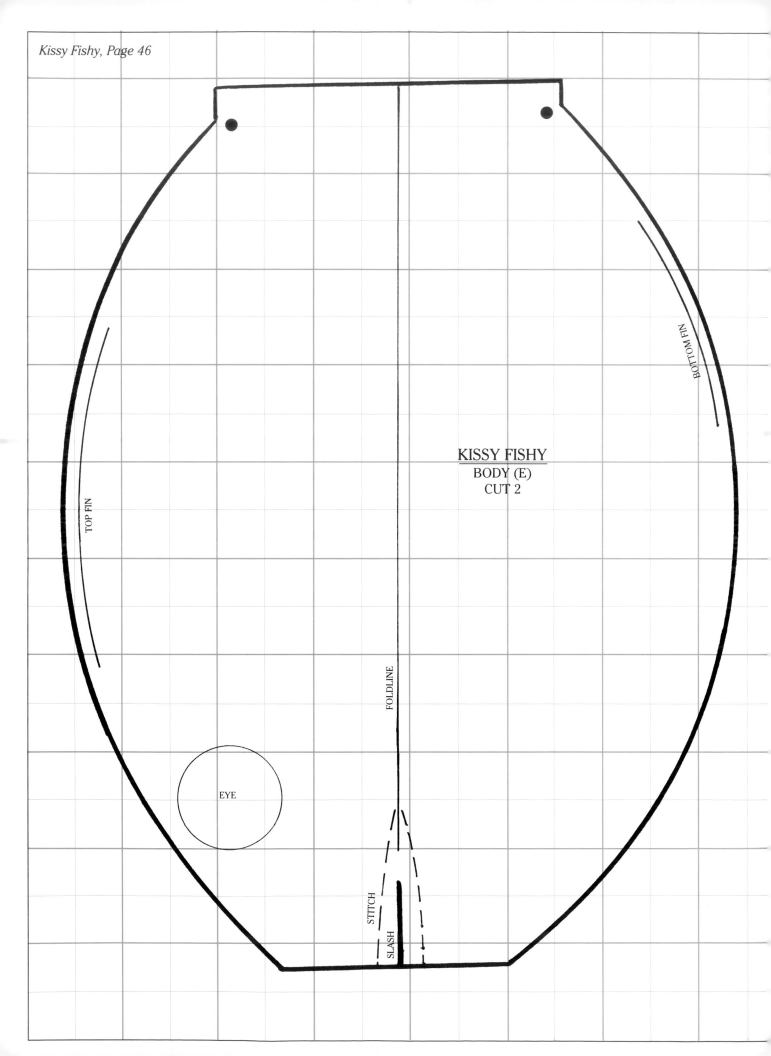

KISSY FISHY
BODY (E)
CUT 2

BOTTOM FIN

TOP FIN

FOLDLINE

EYE

STITCH

SLASH

KISSY FISHY
BOTTOM FIN (B)
CUT 1

FOLDLINE

GATHER

Party Animal

Party Animal is irresistible. Unlike a real cat, he'll cuddle when *you* want. And with his huggable shape, his floppy legs and perky ears, he has an endearing, unco-ordinated quality about him. Invite him to your party. *He'll* always compliment you on the tuna dip.

Make Party Animal in shag or short plush, crazy or neutral colors, leopard, tabby stripes or solids. Even polka dots are great on this cat — the stranger the better. Everyone will comment on this kitty, because it's not instantly obvious what kind of animal it is. Tell people it's Party Animal, your mystery pet.

Party Animal is very easy to make, since none of the legs need to be set in. They are all sewn into the main body seam. Because the face is machine stitched onto the body, there is little handsewing necessary. You can make the feet, tummy and face from a contrasting color, if you wish. Cut the fronts of the ears and the nose from pink fleece or velour. Stuff this pussycat with soft filling, making sure to fill the feet and the face.

Cutting

WHAT YOU NEED

Purchase plush with long, medium or short pile for the body and short pile for the contrasting parts. A soft knit or woven fabric can be used for the ears and nose.

ONE-COLOR PARTY ANIMAL

- 1/2 yd. (.5 m) plush, 36 in. (100 cm) wide
- Scrap, 5 in. (12 cm) square, of pink fleece or velour for ears and nose

TWO-COLOR PARTY ANIMAL

- 1/2 yd. (.5 m) plush, main color, 30 in. (75 cm) wide
- 1/2 yd. (.5 m) plush, contrasting color, 15 in. (40 cm) wide for face, tummy and paws
- Scrap, 5 in. (12 cm) square, pink fleece or velour for ears and nose

STUFFING

- 1/2 lb. (250 g) synthetic filling

NOTIONS

- Two eyes (See page 22 for more information.)

CUTTING REMARKS

- Scale patterns to full size. Pin or trace them onto fabric.
- Position all pattern pieces according to cutting layout. Check whether fabric is single or double thickness and whether patterns are right or wrong side up. (See "Code for Cutting and Sewing".)
- Cut accurately, directly on cutting line.
- Transfer all symbols to wrong side of fabric.
- Cut notches outward.
- Check for nap on pile fabrics. Position nap arrows in direction of nap.

FINISHED SIZE

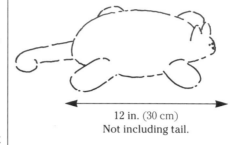

12 in. (30 cm)
Not including tail.

CODE FOR CUTTING AND SEWING

Pink denotes RIGHT side of fabric.

White denotes WRONG side of fabric.

Yellow denotes RIGHT side of pattern.

Dots denote WRONG side of pattern.

CUTTING LAYOUT

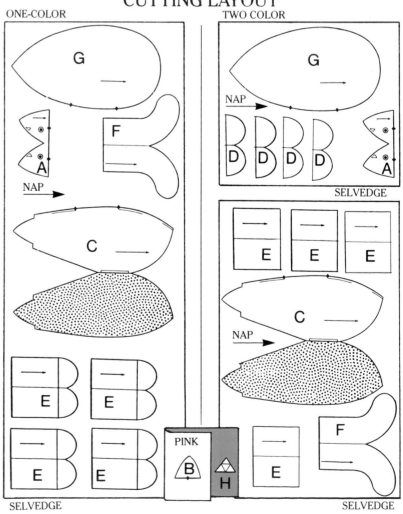

ONE-COLOR

TWO COLOR

Sewing

KNOW BEFORE YOU SEW

- PINS – Use bead-headed pins for visibility and easy retrieval.
- SEAMS – Make seams ¹/₄ in. (.5 cm) wide.
- STITCH – Sew medium-length machine stitches.
- BASTE – Sew long machine stitches. Baste all seams before sewing.

Notch curve.   Clip curve.   Clip corner.

- NOTCH CURVE – Cut V's to seam, evenly along curve.
- CLIP CURVE – Clip to seam, evenly along inside curve.
- CLIP CORNER – Clip from inside corner to pivot in seam.
- REINFORCING – Reinforce all stress points with an extra seam.
- STUFFING – Stuff small areas firmly and larger areas less firmly.
- LADDER STITCH – Sew an invisible seam from the right side.

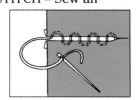

For more information on these or any other sewing terms, consult the glossary at the back of the book.

Face

1 Fold FACE (A) section in half with right sides together. Stitch center seam from fold-edge to end.

Optional: If the pile is long, you may wish to shear the face and paws now, before sewing the cat together. Hold section on your hand and cut pile with scissors held flat. Cut roughly first. Then trim evenly.

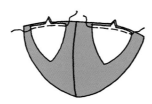

2 Position EAR (B) sections on face section with right sides together, matching single notches. Stitch on seam line. Set aside.

Back

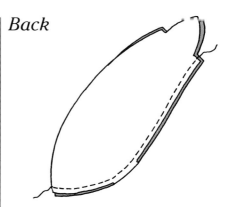

1 Fold BACK (C) section in half with right sides together. Stitch center seam, including fold-edge. Notch curve.

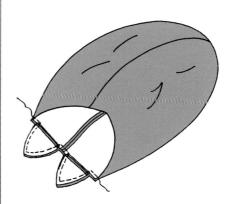

2 Lay back section flat with RIGHT SIDE UP. Position face section on back section with right sides together, matching ears and center seams. Stitch full seam around ears, pivoting at corners and points. Trim points and clip corners. Turn ears right-side-out. Set aside.

Legs

1 *Optional:* For contrasting paws, position one PAW (D) section onto the end of one LEG (E) section with right sides together. Stitch. Repeat for all legs and paws.

2 Fold one LEG (E) section in half with right sides together. Stitch from fold-edge around curve and to end. Notch curve. Turn right-side-out. Repeat with remaining three legs.

3 Stuff all legs with filling. Baste open end of each leg shut, close to raw edge. Set legs aside.

Tail

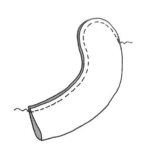

1 Fold TAIL (F) section in half with right sides together. Stitch from fold-edge around curve and to end. Clip inside curve. Turn right-side-out. Stuff tail with filling. Baste open end shut, close to raw edge.

Body

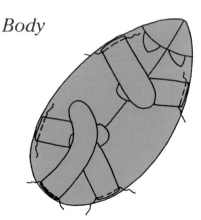

1 Lay back section flat with RIGHT SIDE UP. Position tail and four legs on RIGHT SIDE of back. See pattern for placement. Pin well. Baste close to raw edge.

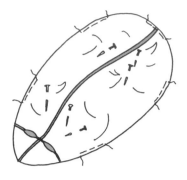

2 Position tail and legs in center of back. Pin in place to prevent them from catching in next seam, step 3. Pin only on wrong side of back section. This will make pins easier to retrieve and to see when sewing.

3 Position TUMMY (G) section on back section with right sides together. Pin well. Baste near seamline in seam allowance, sewing legs and tail into seam, but keeping ears free. Pivot at point and stop at notches. Leave open between notches for turning and stuffing. Carefully check seam. Stitch on seamline.

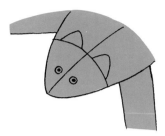

4 Remove all pins and turn right-side-out. Attach eyes. (See page 22 for more information.) Check pattern for placement.

5 Position NOSE (H) section flat with RIGHT SIDE DOWN. Fold in corners, as marked on pattern. Slip stitch nose onto Party Animal's face. See pattern for placement.

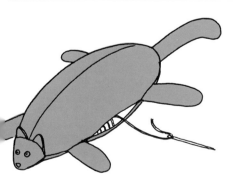

6 Stuff pussycat with filling. Make sure to stuff filling into face. Using heavy thread, doubled, close the side opening with ladder stitch.

Snapshot, 1960.

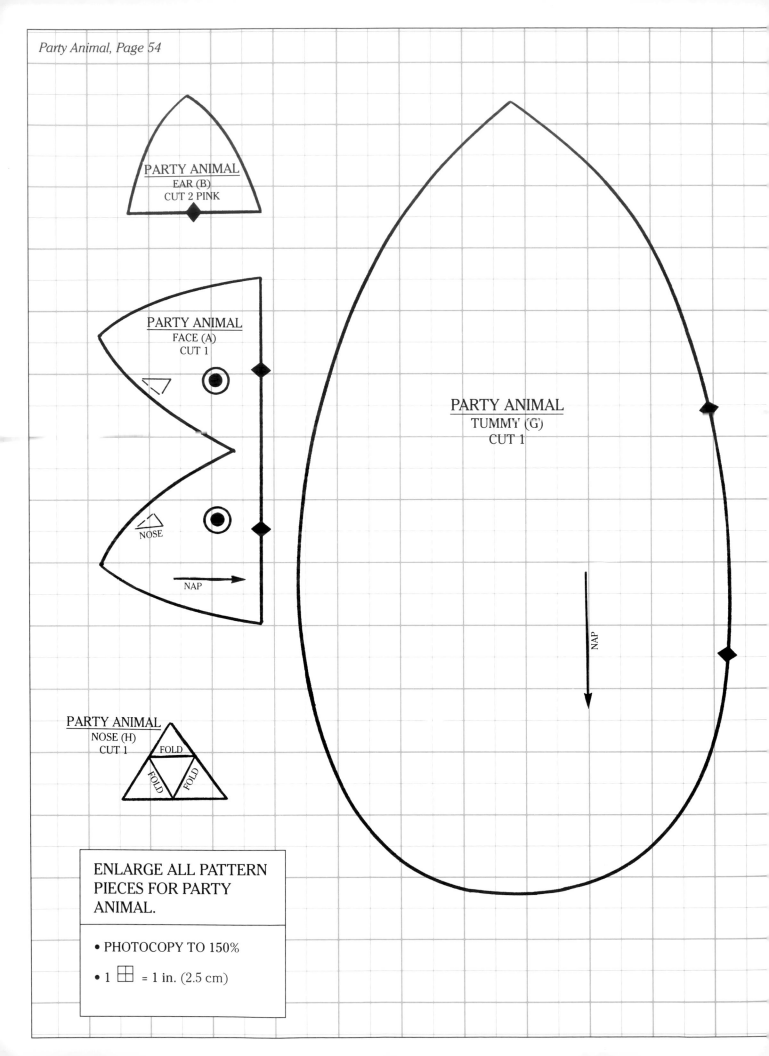

PARTY ANIMAL
EAR (B)
CUT 2 PINK

PARTY ANIMAL
FACE (A)
CUT 1

NOSE

NAP

PARTY ANIMAL
TUMMY (G)
CUT 1

NAP

PARTY ANIMAL
NOSE (H)
CUT 1

FOLD

FOLD

FOLD

ENLARGE ALL PATTERN
PIECES FOR PARTY
ANIMAL.

• PHOTOCOPY TO 150%

• 1 ⊞ = 1 in. (2.5 cm)

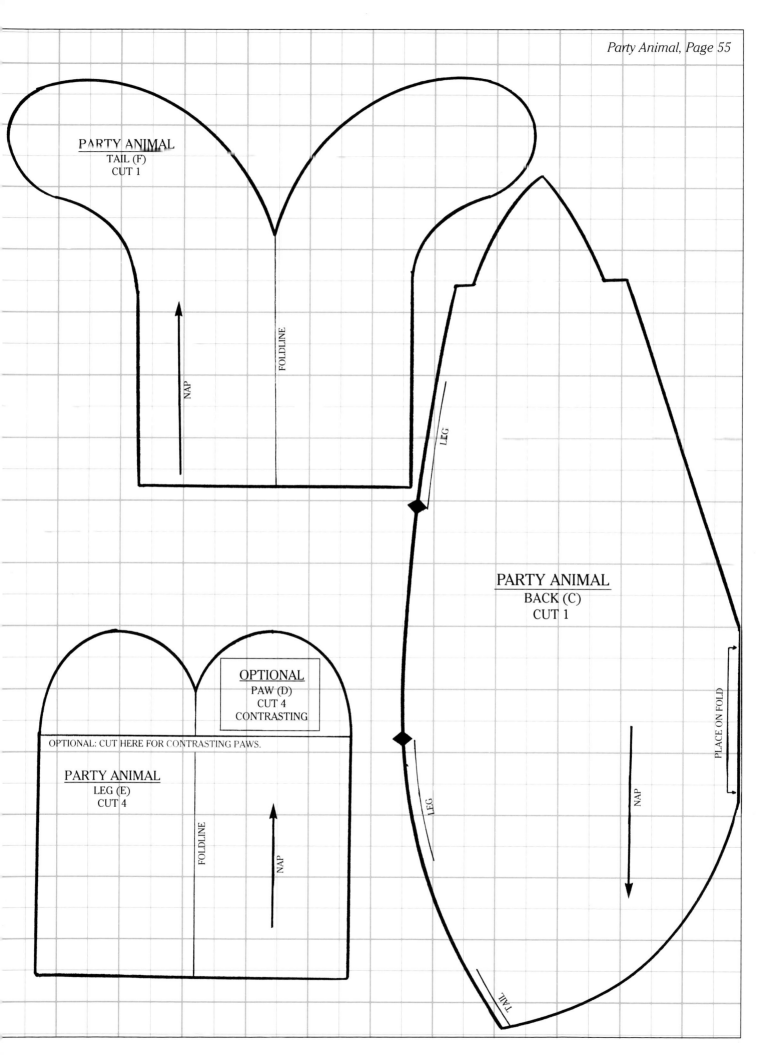

PARTY ANIMAL
TAIL (F)
CUT 1

NAP

FOLDLINE

PARTY ANIMAL
BACK (C)
CUT 1

LEG

LEG

TAIL

NAP

PLACE ON FOLD

OPTIONAL
PAW (D)
CUT 4
CONTRASTING

OPTIONAL: CUT HERE FOR CONTRASTING PAWS.

PARTY ANIMAL
LEG (E)
CUT 4

FOLDLINE

NAP

Caterpillar

Take a lowly worm to new heights with this plump, colorful caterpillar that can be made to suit any occasion or decor. Do it with color: pastels for baby, screaming neon for the adolescent, patterns and jewel tones to suit any age. Do it with texture: super-soft fleece, fuzzy stretch velour, crunchy textured nylon or decorator chintz and lace.

Make this wiggly guy as long as you like by adding more mid-sections and legs. If you are creating several for a birthday or team party, use iron-on initials — one on each bump to name the child or baseball team. He makes a great mascot.

This is a very fast project, mostly made of straight elasticized seams and lots of easy little feet. The elastic is what gives this caterpillar its loveable scrunchiness. Once you get the hang of working with the elastic, it goes very easily. (See page 21 for information on sewing with elastic.)

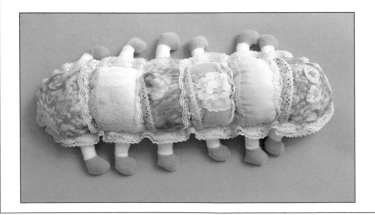

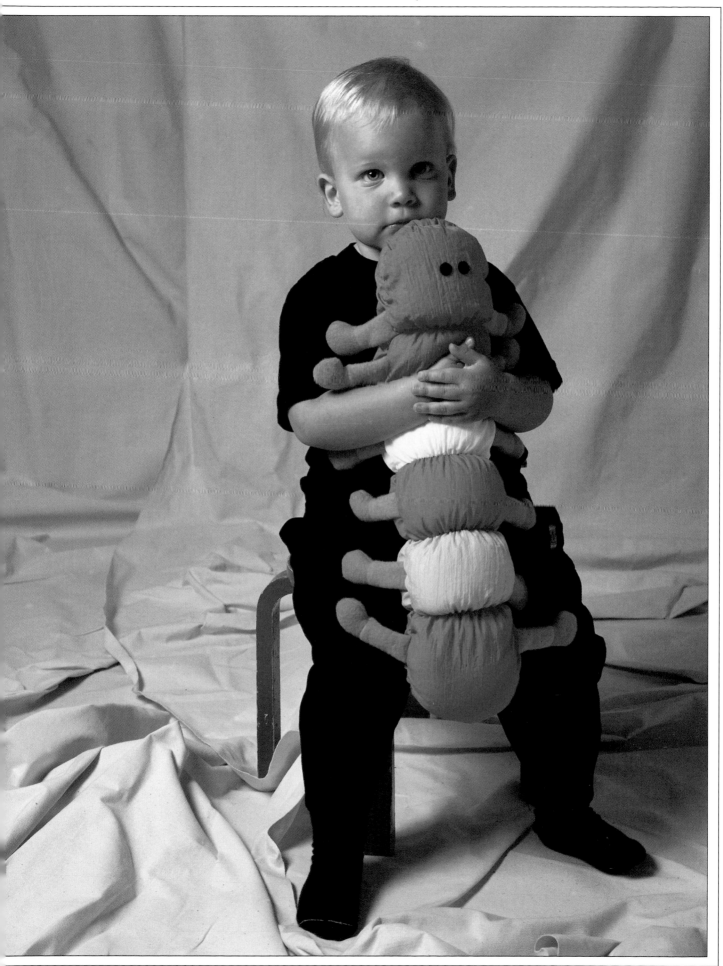

Cutting

WHAT YOU NEED

For the body, a wide range of fabrics are suitable. Purchase stretch knits, such as velour, terry, t-shirting or fleece. Wovens, such as textured nylon, are acceptable if they don't fray easily. Avoid very heavy fabrics and plushes, as they will not respond to the elastic.

For the legs, purchase only stretch fabrics, such as velour, terry, t-shirting or fleece.

CATERPILLAR

- Six different colored fabrics, each ¼ yd. (.25 m), 18 in. (45 cm) wide for body sections, head and tail

- Two different colored stretch fabrics, each ¼ yd. (.25 m), 36 in. (100 cm) wide for legs

STUFFING

- ½ lb. (250 g) synthetic filling

NOTIONS

- Two eyes (See page 22 for more information.)

OPTIONAL

- 3 yd. (3 m) lace

CUTTING REMARKS

- Pin or trace pattern onto fabric.
- Position all pattern pieces according to cutting layout. Check whether fabric is single or double thickness and whether patterns are right or wrong side up. (See "Code for Cutting and Sewing".)
- Cut accurately, directly on cutting line.
- Transfer all symbols to wrong side of fabric.
- Cut notches outward.

- Check stretch fabrics. Position stretch arrows in direction of stretch.

FINISHED SIZE

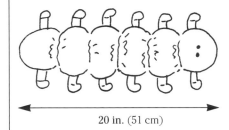

20 in. (51 cm)

CODE FOR CUTTING AND SEWING

 Pink denotes RIGHT side of fabric.

 White denotes WRONG side of fabric.

 Yellow denotes RIGHT side of pattern.

 Dots denote WRONG side of pattern.

CUTTING LAYOUT

FOLD

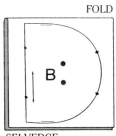

B

SELVEDGE

FOLD

C

SELVEDGE

FOLD

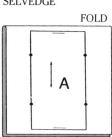

A

SELVEDGE

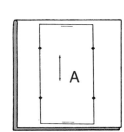

A

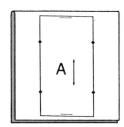

A

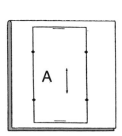

A

STRETCH

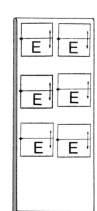

E E
E E
E E

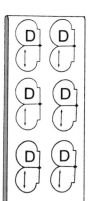

D D
D D
D D

Sewing

KNOW BEFORE YOU SEW

- PINS – Use bead-headed pins for visibility and easy retrieval.
- SEAMS – Make seams $1/4$ in. (.5 cm) wide.
- STITCH – Sew medium-length machine stitches.
- BASTE – Sew long machine stitches. Baste all seams before sewing.

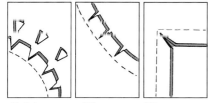

Notch curve.　Clip curve.　Clip corner.

- NOTCH CURVE – Cut V's to seam, evenly along curve.
- CLIP CURVE – Clip to seam, evenly along inside curve.
- CLIP CORNER – Clip from inside corner to pivot in seam.
- REINFORCING – Reinforce all stress points with an extra seam.
- STUFFING – Stuff small areas firmly and larger areas less firmly.
- LADDER STITCH – Sew an invisible seam from the right side.

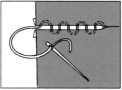

For more information on these or any other sewing terms, consult the glossary at the back of the book.

Body

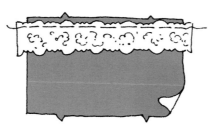

Optional: For a Victorian caterpillar, sew lace into all body seams. Cut lace slightly longer than seam. On the RIGHT SIDE of section, position lace on seam edge. Baste close to raw edge. Sew seam as directed. Repeat for all seams except for legs and feet.

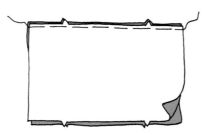

1 Position two BUMPS (A) sections with right sides together, matching notches. Baste one notched edge close to raw edge.

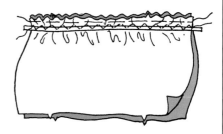

2 Position elastic on seamline next to basting. Stitch seam, while stretching elastic.

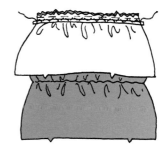

3 Open out the two bumps sections. Lay flat with RIGHT SIDE UP. Position another bumps section onto one of the bumps with right sides together, matching notches. Baste close to raw edge. Sew seam with stretched elastic.

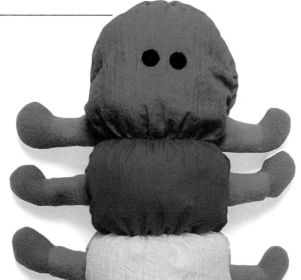

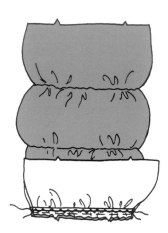

4 Repeat step 3. Now you have four bumps sections sewn together.

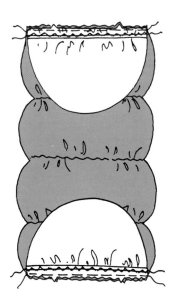

5 Position one HEAD (B) section onto one end of bumps with right sides together, matching notches. Baste notched edge. Sew with stretched elastic.

Repeat with one TAIL (C) section on remaining end of bumps. Now you have the top half of the caterpillar's body.

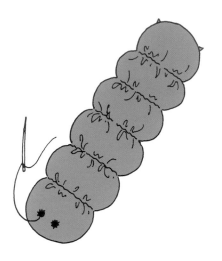

6 Attach Caterpillar's eyes, using pattern for placement. (See page 22 for more information.) Remember, the head section has no notches. Set aside.

7 Make Caterpillar's tummy by repeating steps 1 through 5 with remaining bumps, head and tail sections. Set aside.

Legs and Feet

1 Position one FOOT (D) section onto one LEG (E) section with right sides together, matching single notch. Stitch single-notched edge. Repeat for all leg and foot sections.

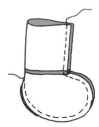

2 Fold one leg-foot section in half with right sides together, matching seams. Starting at fold-edge on foot, stitch around foot and along side of leg. Leave end open for turning and stuffing. Repeat for all leg sections.

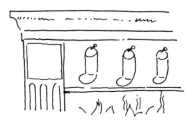

3 *Optional:* Hang on fireplace on Christmas Eve for pet mice.

4 Turn all legs right-side-out. Stuff feet firmly. The handle of a wooden spoon will help to get filling into feet. This will make feet hang down nicely. Stuff legs only lightly with filling. Baste ends of legs shut.

Finishing

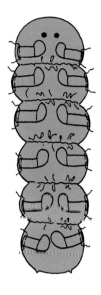

1 Lay body section flat with RIGHT SIDE UP. Position legs on body, using pattern for placement. Be certain that feet are all POINTING TOWARD HEAD. Baste legs in place, close to raw edge.

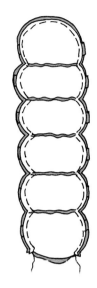

2 Position body sections with right sides together, matching seams and notches on tail. Baste close to raw edge, ending at notches on tail section. Leave open between notches for turning and stuffing.

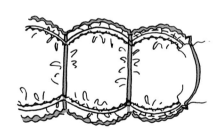

3 Stretch and sew elastic along seamline next to basting, ending at notches in tail section. Leave open between notches.

4 Turn Caterpillar right-side-out. Stuff with filling. You may need to gather Caterpillar like a stocking to get filling into head.

5 Fold in seam allowances on tail opening and close with ladder stitch.

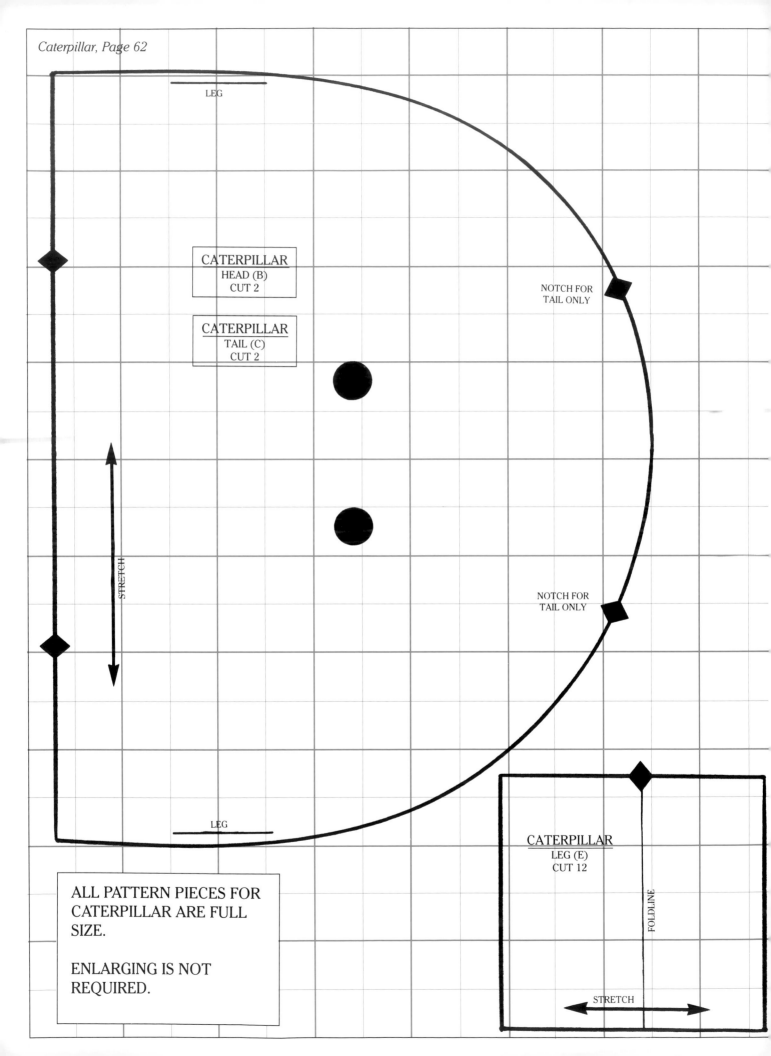

Caterpillar, Page 62

LEG

CATERPILLAR
HEAD (B)
CUT 2

CATERPILLAR
TAIL (C)
CUT 2

NOTCH FOR
TAIL ONLY

STRETCH

NOTCH FOR
TAIL ONLY

LEG

CATERPILLAR
LEG (E)
CUT 12

FOLDLINE

STRETCH

ALL PATTERN PIECES FOR
CATERPILLAR ARE FULL
SIZE.

ENLARGING IS NOT
REQUIRED.

LEG

CATERPILLAR
BUMPS (A)
CUT 2 EACH
OF 4 COLORS,
8 PIECES.

STRETCH

STRETCH

FOLDLINE

LEG

CATERPILLAR
FOOT (D)
CUT 12

Teddy

U niversally recognized as *the* lifelong toy, the Teddy bear has become a lasting symbol of childhood. It is loved by children and adults alike and coveted by collectors who work themselves into a bear-frenzy with all types of Teddy events: Teddy bear picnics, flea markets, Teddy auctions, bear calendars, books and magazines, antique fairs and more.

The Teddy has its own history. It became the namesake of the 26th president of the United States, the very popular Theodore "Teddy" Roosevelt, after a story appeared recounting how the president, on a bear hunt, had refused to shoot a bear cub which had been tied to a tree to ensure the president would not go home empty handed. The original Teddy bear, made in 1902, lives in a glass case in the Smithsonian Institute in Washington D.C.

The nicely proportioned Teddy bear featured here is certain to be any child's well-worn love object or a classic decorative addition for a traditional bedroom. Simplified pattern pieces and construction techniques make this Teddy a rewarding, fast project. Extra-soft plush and filling are bear necessities for this Teddy. While this bear is wonderful in one color, it can be accented with pink or contrasting paw pads and ear fronts made in a different texture or type of fabric such as a knit.

Cutting

WHAT YOU NEED

Purchase the softest, best quality plush available. This Teddy is excellent in virtually any length of pile in any design or color. Choose short pile or a different type of fabric for contrasting parts, or shear the pile for a different texture.

ONE-COLOR TEDDY

- 1/2 yd. (.5 m) plush, 48 in. (120 cm) wide

TWO-COLOR TEDDY

- 1/2 yd. (.5 m) plush for main body, 48 in. (120 cm) wide
- Scrap, 10 in. (25 cm) square, pink plush for ears and paws

STUFFING

- 1 lb. (500 g) synthetic filling

NOTION

- Two eyes (See page 22 for more information.)

OPTIONAL

- Black six-strand embroidery thread for nose

CUTTING REMARKS

- Scale patterns to full size. Pin or trace them onto fabric.
- Position all pattern pieces according to cutting layout. Check whether fabric is single or double thickness and whether patterns are right or wrong side up. (See "Code for Cutting and Sewing".)
- Cut accurately, directly on cutting line.
- Transfer all symbols to wrong side of fabric.
- Check for nap on pile fabrics. Position nap arrows in direction of nap.

FINISHED SIZE

16 in. (40 cm)

CODE FOR CUTTING AND SEWING

Pink denotes RIGHT side of fabric.

White denotes WRONG side of fabric.

Yellow denotes RIGHT side of pattern.

Dots denote WRONG side of pattern.

CUTTING LAYOUT

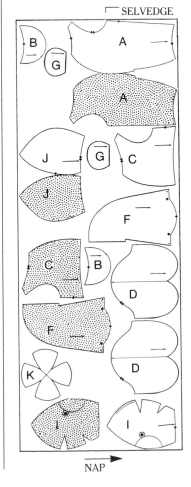

ONE-COLOR TEDDY

TWO-COLOR TEDDY

SELVEDGE

NAP

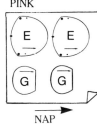

PINK

NAP

Sewing

KNOW BEFORE YOU SEW

- PINS – Use bead-headed pins for visibility and easy retrieval.
- SEAMS – Make seams 1/4 in. (.5 cm) wide.
- STITCH – Sew medium-length machine stitches.
- BASTE – Sew long machine stitches. Baste all seams before sewing.

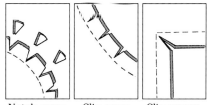

Notch curve.   Clip curve.   Clip corner.

- NOTCH CURVE – Cut V's to seam, evenly along curve.
- CLIP CURVE – Clip to seam, evenly along inside curve.
- CLIP CORNER – Clip from inside corner to pivot in seam.
- REINFORCING – Reinforce all stress points with an extra seam.
- STUFFING – Stuff small areas firmly and larger areas less firmly.
- LADDER STITCH – Sew an invisible seam from the right side.

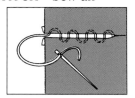

For more information on these or any other sewing terms, consult the glossary at the back of the book.

Body

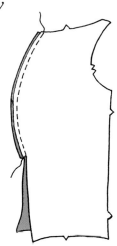

1 Position two FRONT (A) sections with right sides together. Stitch center seam. Stop at crotch, leaving legs free. Notch curve.

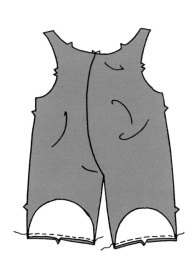

2 Position one PAW (B) section onto end of one front leg with right sides together, matching single notches. Stitch. Repeat with remaining paw section.

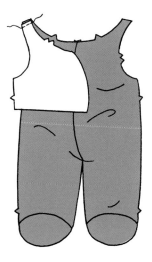

3 Position one BACK (C) section onto front section with right sides together. Match shoulders. Stitch shoulder seam. Reinforce with second seam. Repeat with remaining back section.

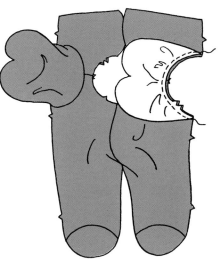

4 Open out body at shoulders and lay flat with RIGHT SIDE UP. Position one ARM (D) section onto armhole with right sides together. Place small ● on shoulder seam and match double notches. Baste, then stitch. Clip inside curve. Repeat with remaining arm section.

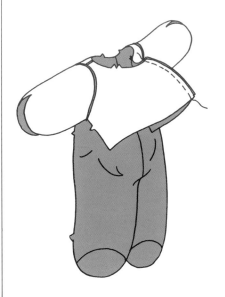

5 Position two back sections with right sides together. Stitch centre seam.

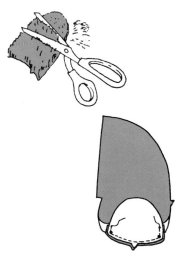

6 Shear two (pink) PAW PAD (E) sections if necessary. Position one paw pad section onto end of one BUM (F) section with right sides together. Match single notches, small •s and large ●s.

Stitch between small •s, pivoting at large ●s. Repeat with remaining paw pad.

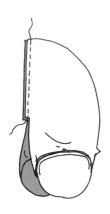

7 Position two bum sections with right sides together. Stitch center seam ending at crotch.

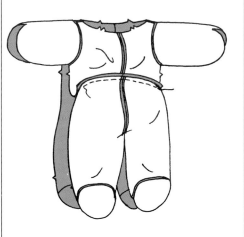

8 Position bum section onto lower edge of back section with right sides together. Match center seam. Working from center seam outwards, pin. Baste, then stitch.

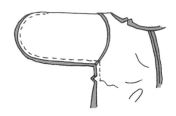

9 Fold one arm section in half with right sides together. Stitch from fold-edge to notch under arm, pivoting at underarm seam.

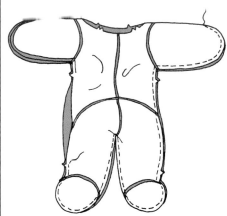

10 Position back onto front with right sides together. Match underarm seams, foot seams, crotch seams and notches. Beginning at fold-edge at top of arm, baste, pivoting at underarm and crotch seams, and ending at notch in far lower leg. Leave side seam open for turning and stuffing. Check seam thoroughly. Stitch. Turn right-side-out. Admire. Set aside.

Head

1 Shear two (pink) EAR (C) sections if necessary. Position two ear sections, (one pink) with right sides together. Stitch curved edge. Notch curve. Turn right-side-out. Baste straight edge closed. Repeat with remaining ear sections.

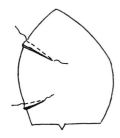

2 Stitch four darts in FACE (I) sections.

3 Position two face sections with right sides together. Stitch center seam.

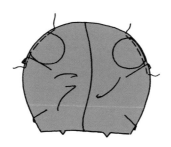

4 Open out face section and lay RIGHT SIDE UP. Position ears with sheared-side-down on face, aligning outside edge of ears with large darts. Baste ears in place. Continue basting to tack large darts away from ears.

5 Position two HEAD (J) sections with right sides together, matching single notches. Stitch single-notched edge.

6 Position head section onto face section with right sides together. Stitch curved edge, sewing ears into seam. Since small children love to use the ears of Teddy as handles, reinforce with second seam, close to first seam.

7 Fold NOSE (K) section in half with right sides together. Stitch full center seam, including fold-edge. Repeat for cross seam. Notch curves.

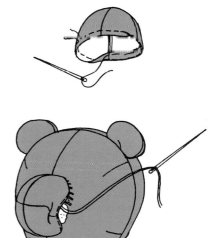

8 Baste along seamline around raw edges of nose section. Turn raw edge under along basting. Using long stitches, hand tack.
Stuff nose with filling and position nose onto face of Teddy. See pattern for placement. Using heavy thread, doubled, ladder stitch nose into place, picking up basting stitches on nose for an even edge.

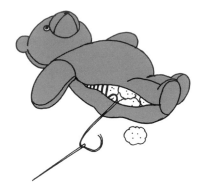

9 Attach eyes. (See page 22 for more information.) See pattern for placement.

Optional: Create nose with satin stitch or with commercial nose. (See page 25 for more information.)

11 Turn bear right-side-out through side opening. Stuff with filling. Head, legs and arms should be stuffed firmly, while body should be softer. To make bear sit up and to allow legs to swing, place very little stuffing at tops of legs.

Using heavy thread, doubled, close side opening with ladder stitch.

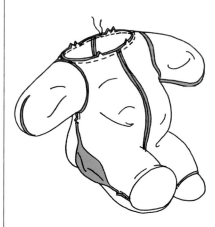

10 Turn body WRONG-SIDE-OUT. With head RIGHT-SIDE-OUT, place head inside body with right sides together. Match raw edge of neck opening with raw edge of head. Match notches and seams. Check that face is toward front. Pin well. Baste. Stitch neck seam.

12 Cuddle time.

Studio Portrait, 1936.

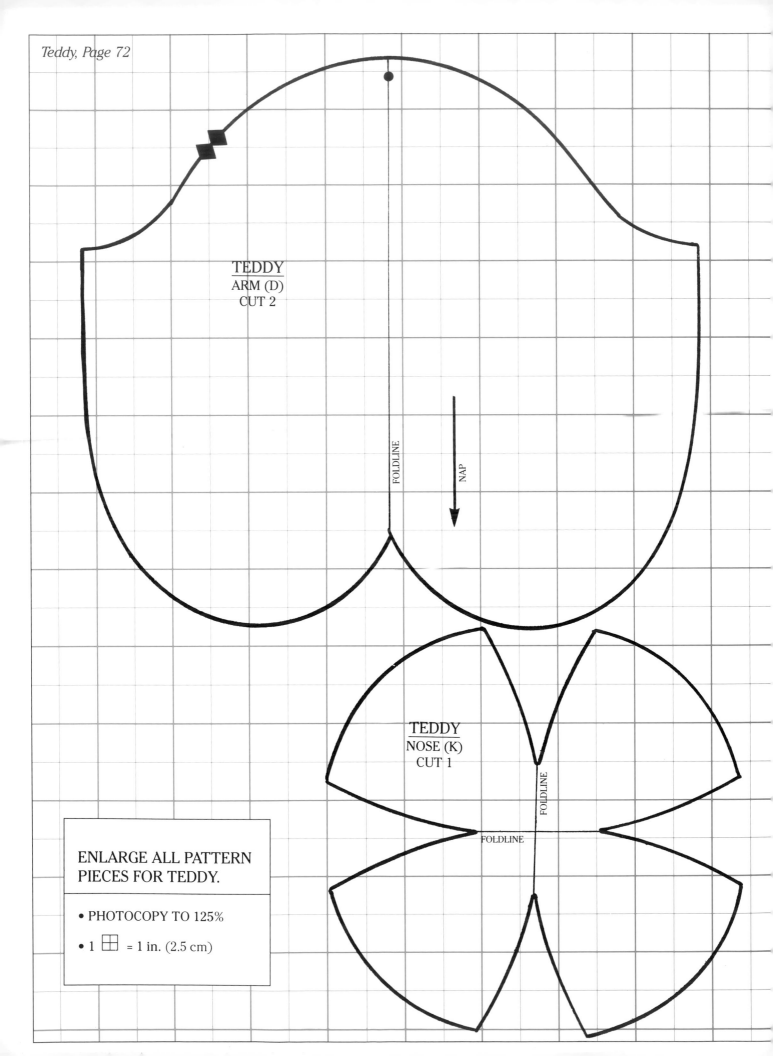

TEDDY
ARM (D)
CUT 2

FOLDLINE

NAP

TEDDY
NOSE (K)
CUT 1

FOLDLINE

FOLDLINE

ENLARGE ALL PATTERN
PIECES FOR TEDDY.

• PHOTOCOPY TO 125%

• 1 ⊞ = 1 in. (2.5 cm)

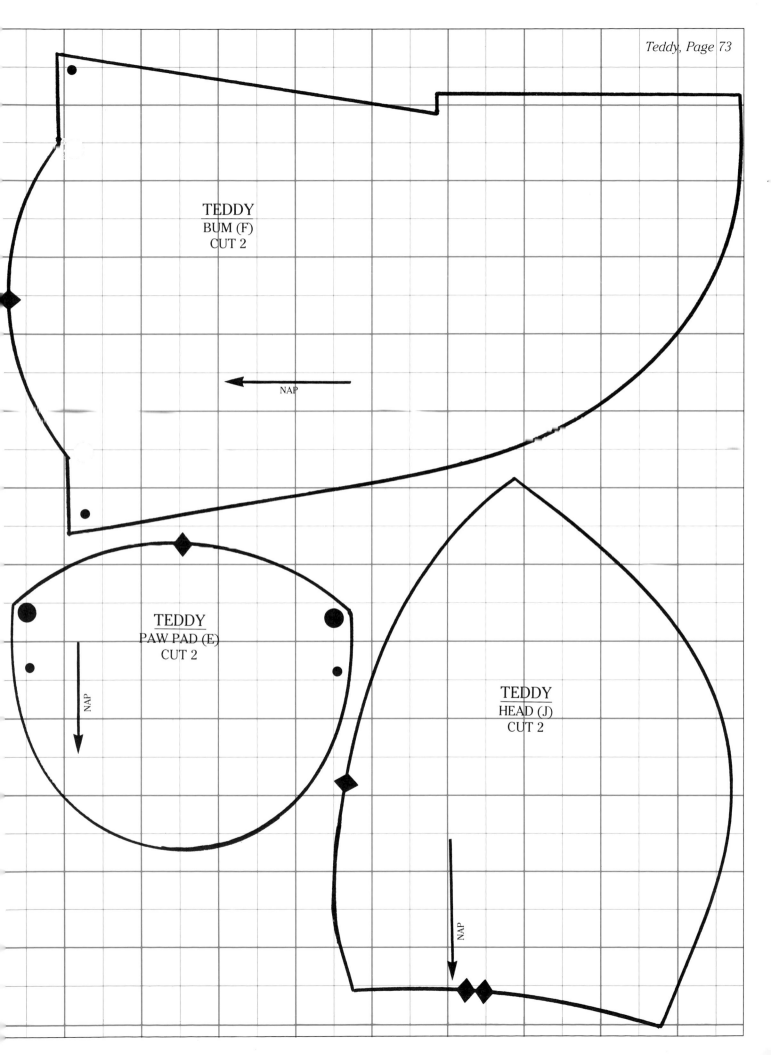

TEDDY
BUM (F)
CUT 2

NAP

TEDDY
PAW PAD (E)
CUT 2

NAP

TEDDY
HEAD (J)
CUT 2

NAP

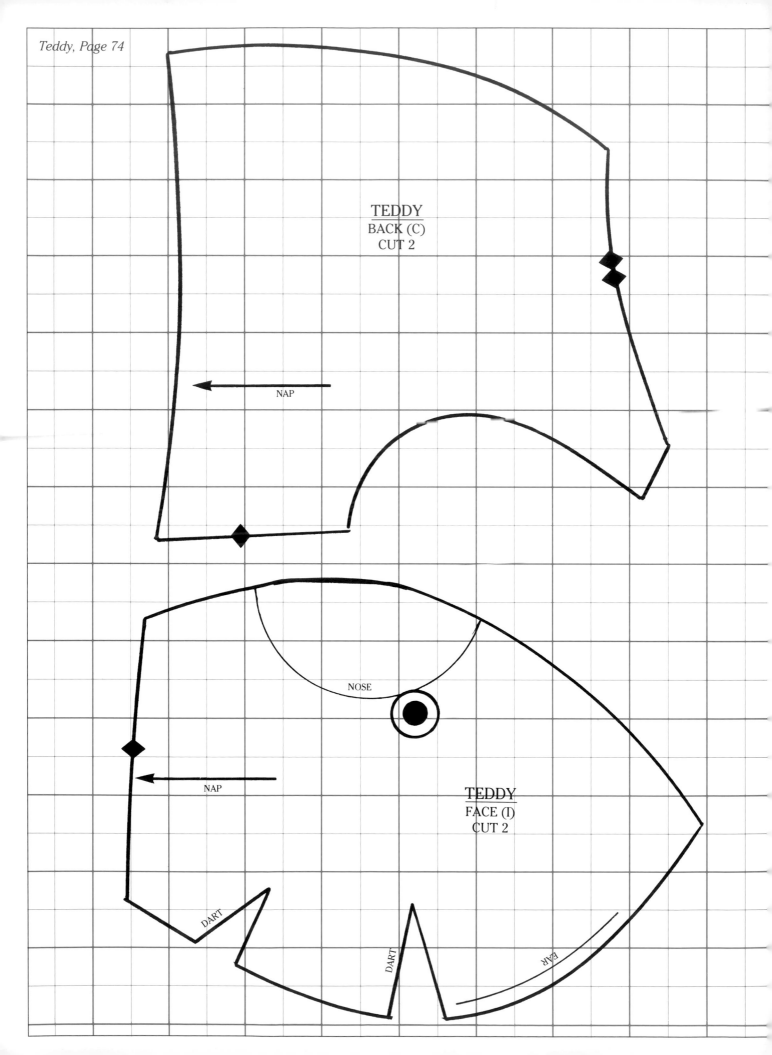

TEDDY
BACK (C)
CUT 2

NAP

TEDDY
FACE (I)
CUT 2

NOSE

NAP

DART

DART

EAR

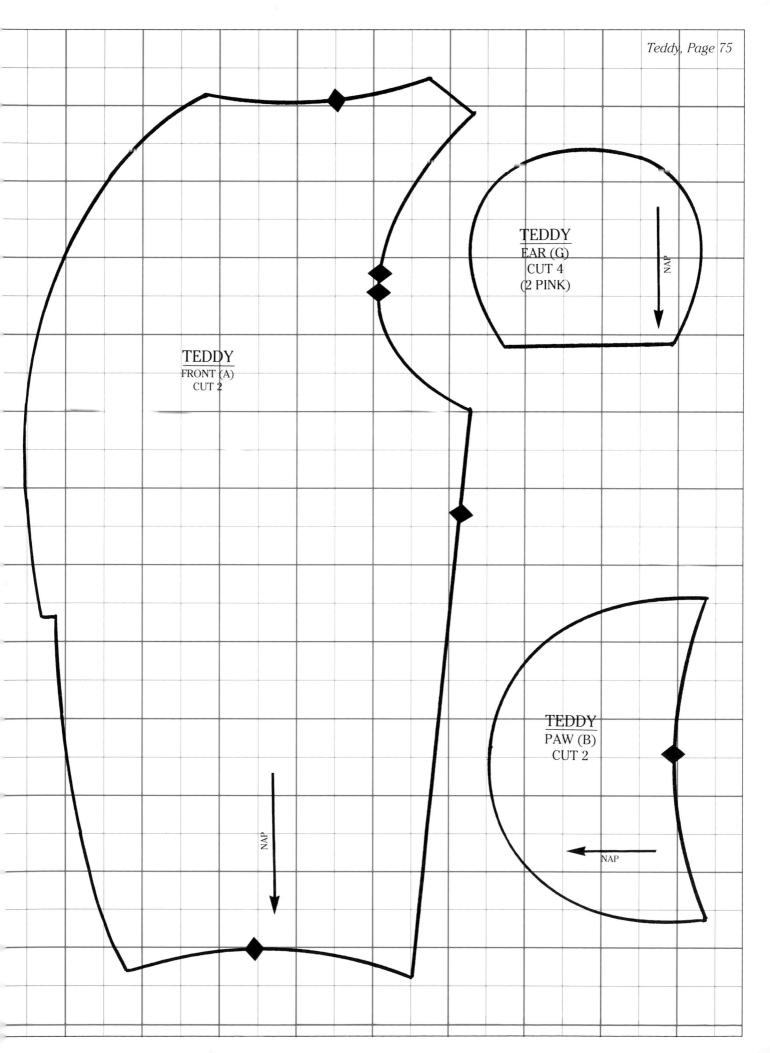

TEDDY
EAR (G)
CUT 4
(2 PINK)

NAP

TEDDY
FRONT (A)
CUT 2

NAP

TEDDY
PAW (B)
CUT 2

NAP

Monster

Meet Hugbert, the somewhat worried looking, but personable monster with non-working parts — feet too big, wings too small, three-toed hands and a snaggled buck-toothed frown. The result adds up to an extremely loveable, snugable guy with unruly hair and a penchant for chocolate coated sardines, which he often sneaks at night while everyone's asleep.

Hugbert is the perfect monster for all kids who are absolutely positive that there is something evil lurking in the closet or under the bed, because Hugbert is the friendly monster that guards and protects small sleeping children from nasties in the night.

Hugbert is a very rewarding, large project that can be made quickly and easily. His accessories — arms, wings, horns, teeth — are optional. You may wish to experiment with some of your own. Try to get extra-soft filling for Hugbert. The squashier you make him, the more endearing he will be.

Cutting

WHAT YOU NEED

Purchase plush with short to medium length pile for the body and long pile (shag) for the head. Choose stretch velour or a similar stretch fabric, such as fleece, for the legs, arms and eyelids. A heavy stretch or woven can be used for the beak and a light crisp fabric that frays very little, such as textured nylon, is good for the horns, wings, teeth and eyes.

MONSTER

- 1/2 yd. (.5 m) plush, minimum width 36 in. (100 cm) for body
- 2/3 yd. (.7 m) stretch fabric, velour or similar, minimum width 60 in. (150 cm) for arms and legs
- Remnant, 18 in. (50 cm) square of textured nylon or similar for wings, eyes, teeth and horns
- Remnant, 12 in. (30 cm) square of stretch or woven fabric for beak
- Remnant, 10 in. (25 cm) square of shag plush for head

STUFFING

- 1 lb. (500 g) synthetic filling

NOTIONS

- Thread to match wings for topstitching
- Heavy black thread or embroidery thread for eyes

CUTTING REMARKS

- Scale patterns to full size. Pin or trace them onto fabric.
- Position all pattern pieces according to cutting layout. Check whether fabric is single or double thickness and whether patterns are right or wrong side up. (See "Code for Cutting and Sewing".)
- Cut accurately, directly on cutting line.

- Transfer all symbols to wrong side of fabric.
- Cut notches outward.
- Check for nap on pile fabrics. Position nap arrows in direction of nap.
- Check stretch fabrics. Position stretch arrows in direction of stretch.

FINISHED SIZE

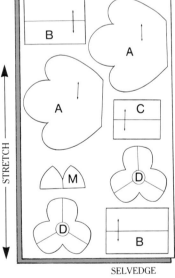

25" (63 cm)

CODE FOR CUTTING AND SEWING

 Pink denotes RIGHT side of fabric.

 White denotes WRONG side of fabric.

 Yellow denotes RIGHT side of pattern.

 Dots denote WRONG side of pattern.

CUTTING LAYOUT

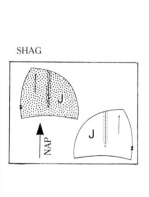

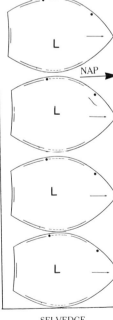

Sewing

KNOW BEFORE YOU SEW

- PINS – Use bead-headed pins for visibility and easy retrieval.
- SEAMS – Make seams 1/4 in. (.5 cm) wide.
- STITCH – Sew medium-length machine stitches.
- BASTE – Sew long machine stitches. Baste all seams before sewing.

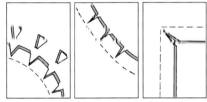

Notch curve.   Clip curve.   Clip corner.

- NOTCH CURVE – Cut V's to seam, evenly along curve.
- CLIP CURVE – Clip to seam, evenly along inside curve.
- CLIP CORNER – Clip from inside corner to pivot in seam.
- REINFORCING – Reinforce all stress points with an extra seam.
- STUFFING – Stuff small areas firmly and larger areas less firmly.
- LADDER STITCH – Sew an invisible seam from the right side.

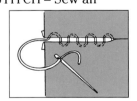

For more information on these or any other sewing terms, consult the glossary at the back of the book.

Legs and Feet

1 Position two TOES (A) sections with right sides together. Stitch around tocs, pivoting at corners. Leave straight edge open. Repeat with remaining toes sections.

Clip corners and notch curves. Turn toes right-side-out.

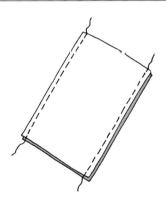

2 Position two LEG (B) sections with right sides together. Stitch both long sides. Leave short ends open. Repeat with remaining leg section.

3 With one toes section RIGHT SIDE OUT and one leg section WRONG SIDE OUT, place leg over toes. They will be right sides together. Match seams. Stitch around opening. Turn right-side-out. Repeat with remaining toes and leg.

4 Stuff toes firmly and legs lightly. Fold one leg along foldlines marked on pattern, matching side seams. Baste end shut. Gather gently. Repeat with remaining leg.

Arms

1 Fold one ARM (C) section in half, lengthwise. Stitch long edge. Turn right-side-out. Repeat with remaining arm section.

2 Position one HAND (D) section, with hole in center, over end of one arm section. Be sure they are right sides together. Stitch around end. Repeat.

Note: Place presser foot INSIDE arm for easier sewing.

3 Turn arm WRONG-SIDE-OUT. Position one hand section, without hole in center, onto one arm/hand section with right sides together. Stitch, pivoting at corners. Clip corners and notch curves. Turn right-side-out through arm. Repeat.

4 Stuff hands very lightly with filling. To form fingers, fold one finger in half along foldline, as marked on pattern. Top stitch from arm-seam to corner. Repeat for all fingers.

Stuff the arms with filling. Baste open ends of arms shut. Set aside.

Accessories

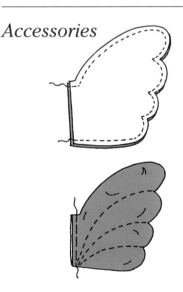

1 Position two WING (F) sections with right sides together. Stitch curved edge. Leave straight edge open for turning and stuffing. Clip corners and notch curves. Turn right-side-out. Stuff very lightly. Baste open edge shut.

Top stitch as marked on pattern. Repeat with remaining wing sections. Set aside.

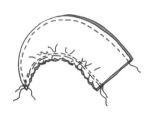

2 Position two HORN (G) sections with right sides together. Baste and gather inside curved edge. Stitch curved edges, pivoting at point. Leave straight edge open for turning and stuffing. Trim point, Turn right-side-out. Stuff lightly and baste straight edge shut. Repeat with remaining horn sections. Set aside.

3 Position two TOOTH (H) sections with right sides together. Stitch two unnotched sides. Trim point. Turn right-side-out. Stuff lightly and baste notched edge shut. Repeat for all remaining tooth sections. Set aside.

Head

1 Position two TOP-BEAK (I) sections with right sides together. Stitch single-notched edge. Set aside.

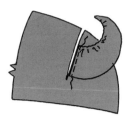

2 Lay one HEAD (J) section flat with RIGHT SIDE UP. Place raw edge of one horn against raw edge of slash in head section. Baste in place, close to raw edge. Repeat with remaining head section and horn.

3 Fold one head section in half, along slash, with right sides together. Stitch slash shut like a dart, sewing horn into seam. Repeat with remaining head section.

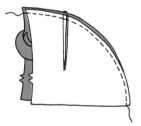

4 Position two head sections with right sides together. Stitch curved center seam, keeping horns free.

5 Position top-beak section onto head with right sides together, matching double notches. Stitch notched edge, keeping horns free. Set aside.

6 Position teeth on right side of BOTTOM BEAK (K) section, matching notches. Baste close to raw edge.

Body

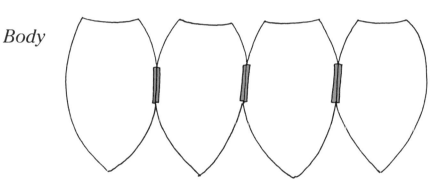

1 Stitch four BODY (L) sections together, with right sides together, at short seamlines, as indicated on pattern. Clip seams at ends of stitching.

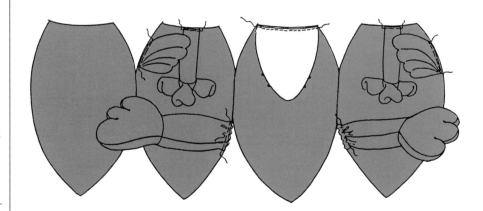

2 Lay body section flat with RIGHT SIDE UP. Position legs, arms, wings and beak bottom sections onto RIGHT SIDE of body section. See pattern and diagram above for placement. Sew beak bottom along seamline. Baste other appendages in place, close to raw edges.

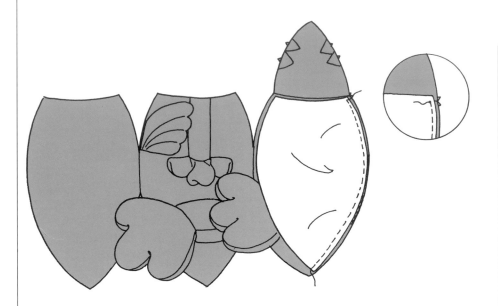

3 Lay body flat with RIGHT SIDE UP. Fold far right panel to left, onto adjoining panel. Stitch far-right curved edge from beak seam to end, including fold area, sewing one leg in seam. Remember to keep the other accessories free. Notch curve.

6 Turn body WRONG-SIDE-OUT. Position head section onto body with right sides together, matching notches and seams. Pin well. Baste. Check seam. Stitch full outer-edge seam.
   Turn right-side-out by pulling legs and body through opening.

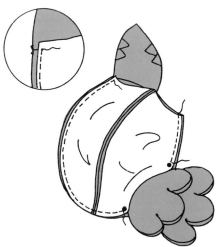

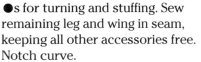

4 Lay body flat with RIGHT SIDE UP. Fold far left panel to right, onto adjoining panel. Stitch far-left curved edge. Sew one wing into seam, keeping other accessories free.

5 Fold body in half with right sides together, matching large ●s and seams. Place legs between large ●s. Stitch curved edge, from large ●s to ends. Leave seam open between large ●s for turning and stuffing. Sew remaining leg and wing in seam, keeping all other accessories free. Notch curve.

7 Stuff monster with filling through opening in back. Pack head and beak firmly and body somewhat more softly.
   Using heavy thread, doubled, close opening with ladder stitch.

Eyes

1 Fold one EYE (M) section in half with right sides together. Stitch center seam, including fold area. Repeat for remaining three sections.

2 Position one white and one contrasting eye section together, matching center seams and notches. Stitch curved edge. Repeat.

3 Baste close to raw edge of one eye section. Gather gently and stuff firmly. Then gather tightly and tie off. Repeat.

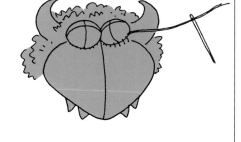

4 Using heavy thread, doubled, sew eyes in place with ladder stitch. See pattern for placement.

5 Using heavy thread, doubled, or black embroidery thread, create black dots on eyes with satin stitch.

6 Stock up on chocolate covered sardines.

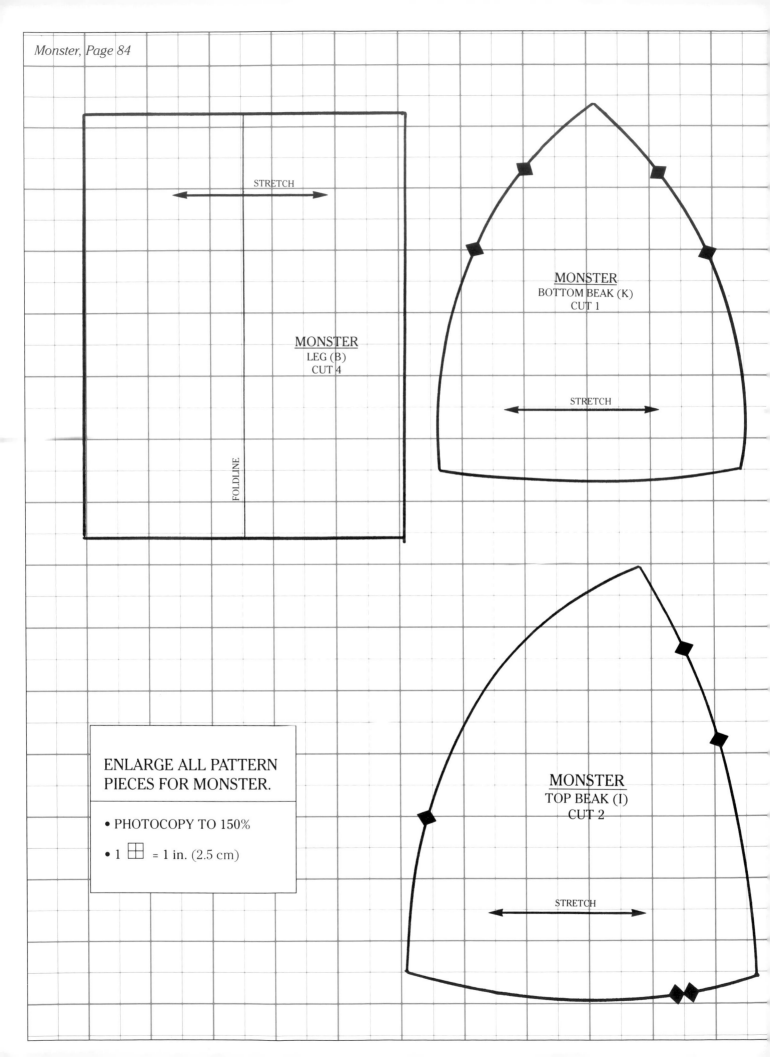

STRETCH

MONSTER
LEG (B)
CUT 4

FOLDLINE

MONSTER
BOTTOM BEAK (K)
CUT 1

STRETCH

ENLARGE ALL PATTERN
PIECES FOR MONSTER.

• PHOTOCOPY TO 150%

• 1 ⊞ = 1 in. (2.5 cm)

MONSTER
TOP BEAK (I)
CUT 2

STRETCH

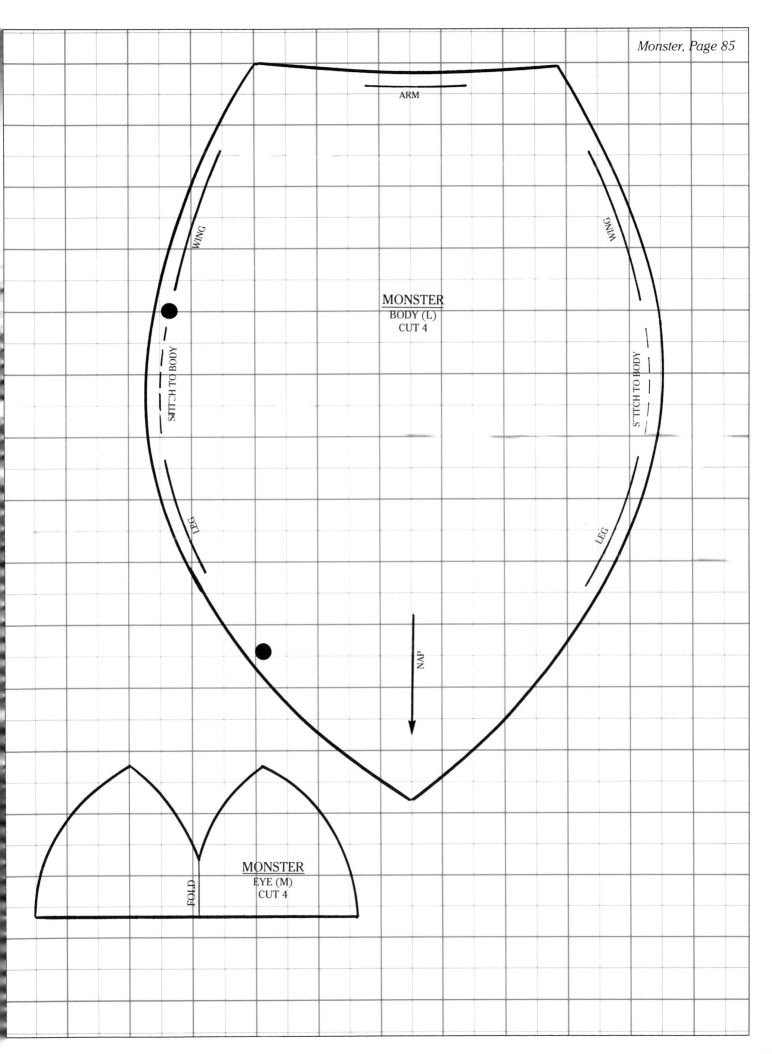

ARM

WING

WING

MONSTER
BODY (L)
CUT 4

STITCH TO BODY

STITCH TO BODY

LEG

LEG

NAP

FOLD

MONSTER
EYE (M)
CUT 4

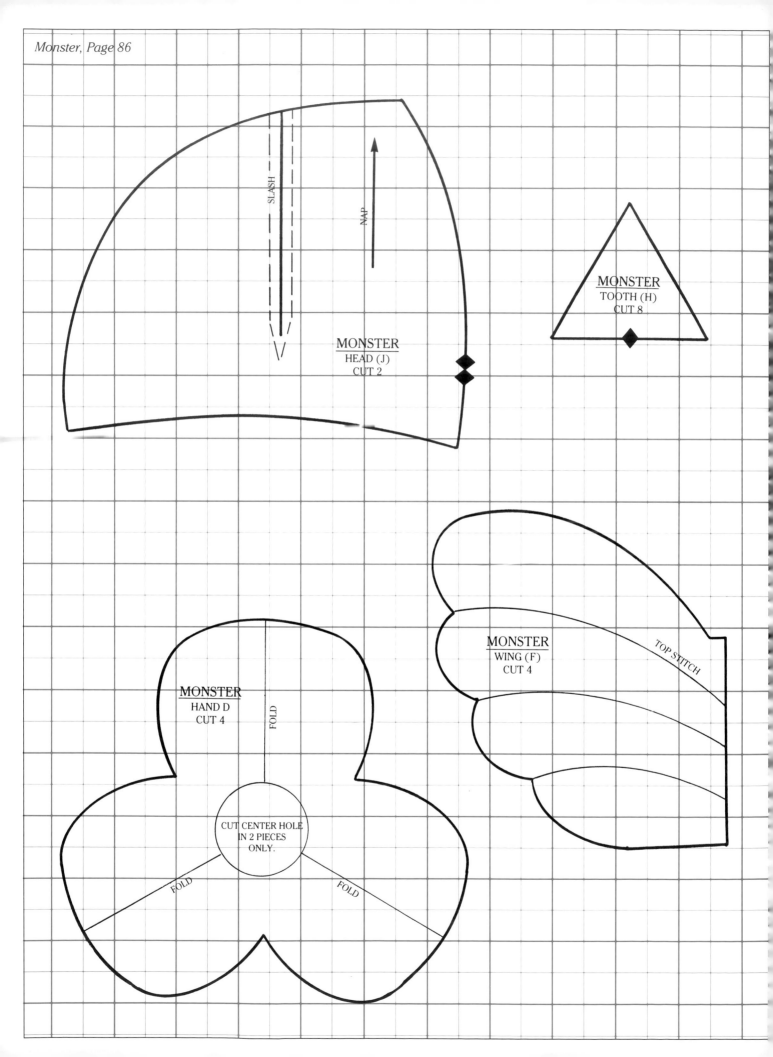

SLASH

NAP

MONSTER
HEAD (J)
CUT 2

MONSTER
TOOTH (H)
CUT 8

MONSTER
WING (F)
CUT 4

TOP STITCH

MONSTER
HAND D
CUT 4

FOLD

FOLD

FOLD

CUT CENTER HOLE
IN 2 PIECES
ONLY.

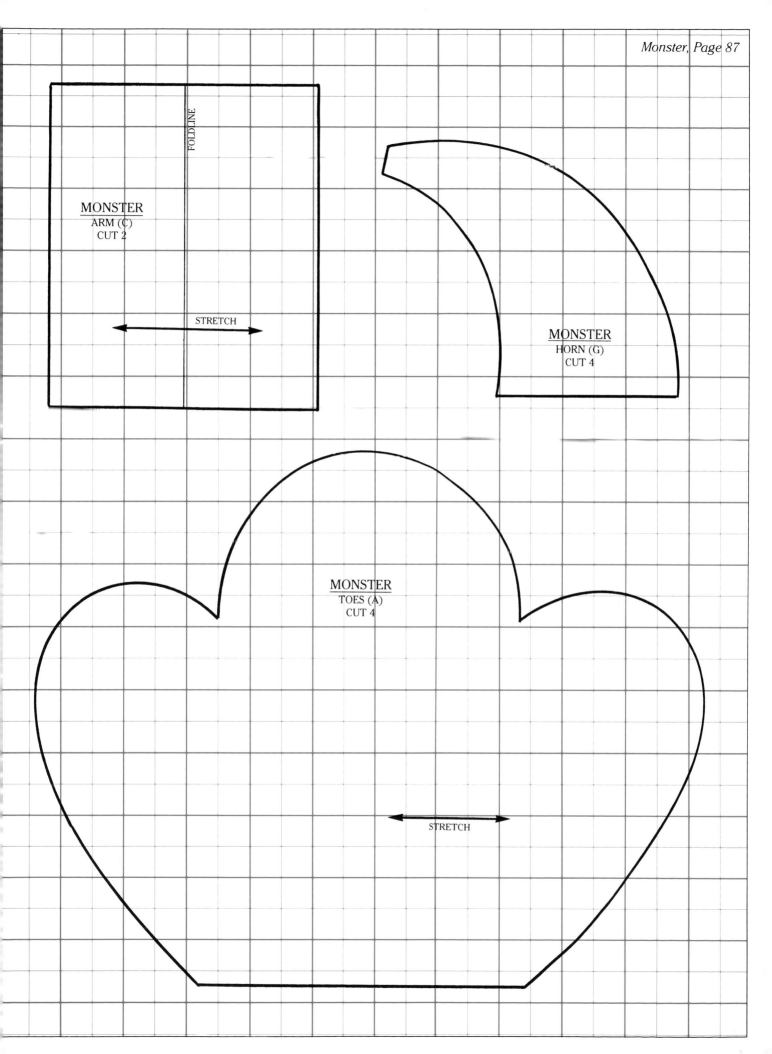

MONSTER
ARM (C)
CUT 2

FOLDLINE

STRETCH

MONSTER
HORN (G)
CUT 4

MONSTER
TOES (A)
CUT 4

STRETCH

Which came first, the chicken or the egg? This perennial question pops up time and again with P.J. Birdy. One minute, it's a round spotted egg, and the next, the egg hatches a fluffy baby bird. When the toy is bird-side-out, it's a great pyjama bag for a small child's p.j.s. Remove the pyjamas by turning the bird egg-side-out and P.J. Birdie sleeps in her egg.

Kids love convertible creatures and P.J. Birdy makes a great birthday gift-within-a-gift with p.j.s. already inside. And don't forget Mother's Day, Father's Day and especially "the better half" at Valentine's Day with a special sweet or naughty surprise tucked inside.

This bird is made in two parts: the egg which is a woven fabric and the bird which is plush and has the wings, head and legs attached. The two parts are then assembled. The results are well worth the effort. So, which did come first, the chicken or the egg?

P.J. Birdy

Head

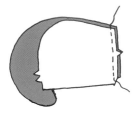

1 Position one HEAD (C) section on one BEAK (D) section with right sides together, matching single notches. Stitch single-notched edge. Repeat with remaining beak and head sections. Lay seams toward beak.

2 Baste CREST (E) section just inside seam allowance, between small ●s. Gather. Position LINING (F) section on WRONG side of crest section with long sides on gathers. Adjust gathers to match length of lining. Stitch gathers to lining.

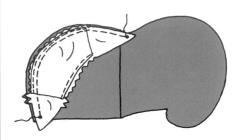

3 Position crest on one head section with right sides together, matching double notches and large ●s. Stitch between large ●s. Repeat so that crest and head sections are all one piece. Stuff filling into crest section. Set aside.

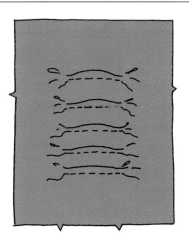

4 Make tucks in NECK (G) section by folding neck section with **WRONG SIDES TOGETHER**, matching tuck lines. Top stitch five tucks.

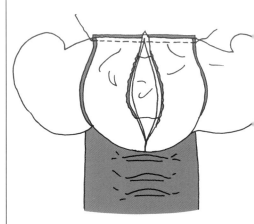

5 Position unnotched edge of neck section on straight edge of head section with right sides together. Stitch.

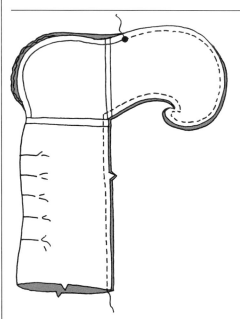

6 Fold head and neck in half with right sides together, matching seams and notches. Stitch from large ● on beak, around beak, then along neck to end. Notch curves. Clip inside curve and inside corner.

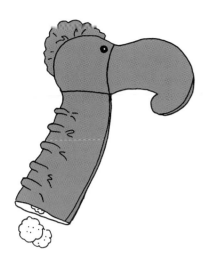

7 Turn head right-side-out. Attach eyes. See pattern for placement. (See page 22 for more information.) Stuff firmly with filling. Baste open end shut, close to raw edge.

Wings

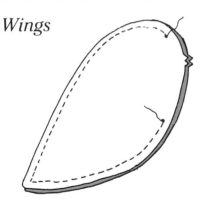

1 Position two WING (H) sections with right sides together. Stitch edge, ending at small •s. Leave open between small •s for turning and stuffing. Clip seam at small •s. Trim point. Notch curves, if necessary. Repeat with remaining wing sections. Set aside.

Body

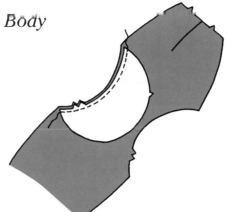

1 Ease stitch all four THIGH (I) sections on seamline along double-notched edge. Gather gently. Sew dart in TUMMY (I) section. Position one thigh section on tummy section with right sides together, matching double notches. Adjust ease stitching to fit. Stitch double-notched edge. Repeat with one remaining thigh section. Set aside.

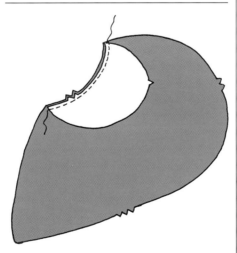

2 Position one thigh section on one SIDE (K) section with right sides together, matching double notches. Adjust ease stitching to fit. Stitch double-notched edge. Repeat with remaining thigh and side sections. Set aside.

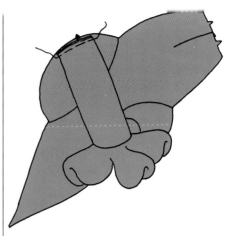

3 Position one leg section on RIGHT SIDE of tummy section, matching single notches. Baste close to raw edge. Repeat with remaining leg section.

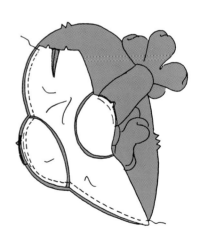

4 Position one side section on tummy section with right sides together, matching thighs and single notches.
   Stitch full side seam of tummy section, pivoting at thigh seams. Sew leg into seam. Repeat with remaining side section. Set aside.

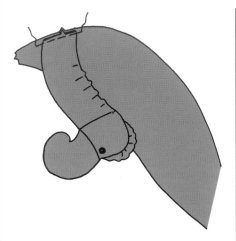

5 Position neck on RIGHT SIDE of one BACK (L) section matching single notch. Baste close to raw edge.

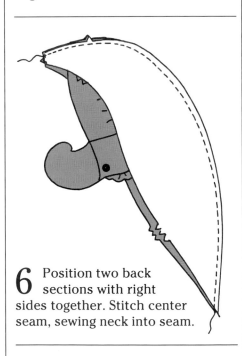

6 Position two back sections with right sides together. Stitch center seam, sewing neck into seam.

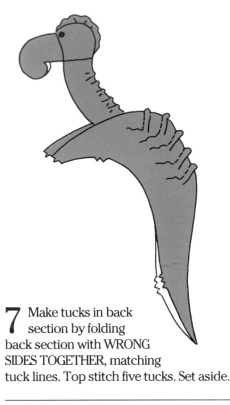

7 Make tucks in back section by folding back section with WRONG SIDES TOGETHER, matching tuck lines. Top stitch five tucks. Set aside.

8 Position one wing on RIGHT SIDE of one side section, between small •s, matching double notches. Baste close to raw edge. Repeat with remaining wing section.

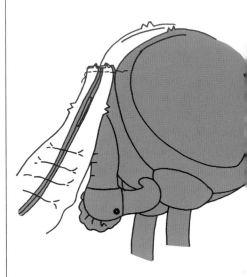

9 Position back section on tummy section with right sides together, matching notches and placing center seam on dart. Stitch edge.

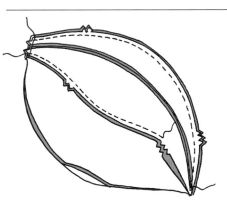

10 Turn body WRONG-SIDE-OUT. Position back section on one side section with right sides together, matching double and triple notches. Stitch one full side seam.
Repeat, ending at triple notch. Leave open between triple notch and tail for turning and stuffing.

11 Stuff body with filling. Be sure to get some filling into thighs. Ladder stitch opening shut.

Collar

1 Buzz needs a collar to help hold his head up. Position two COLLAR (M) sections with right sides together. Stitch inside curve of collar. Do not clip curve.

Baste outside curve of collar. Gather gently. Stay stitch gathers. Turn right-side-out.

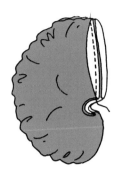

2 Fold collar section in half. It will be right sides together. Position two inside raw edges with right sides together. Stitch.

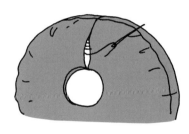

3 Stuff collar firmly through opening. Ladder stitch opening shut.

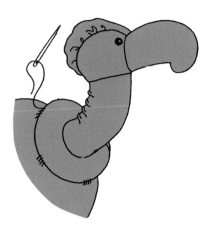

4 Force collar over buzzard's head and to base of neck. Hand tack securely in three or four places.

5 Set up a nice perch for Buzz.

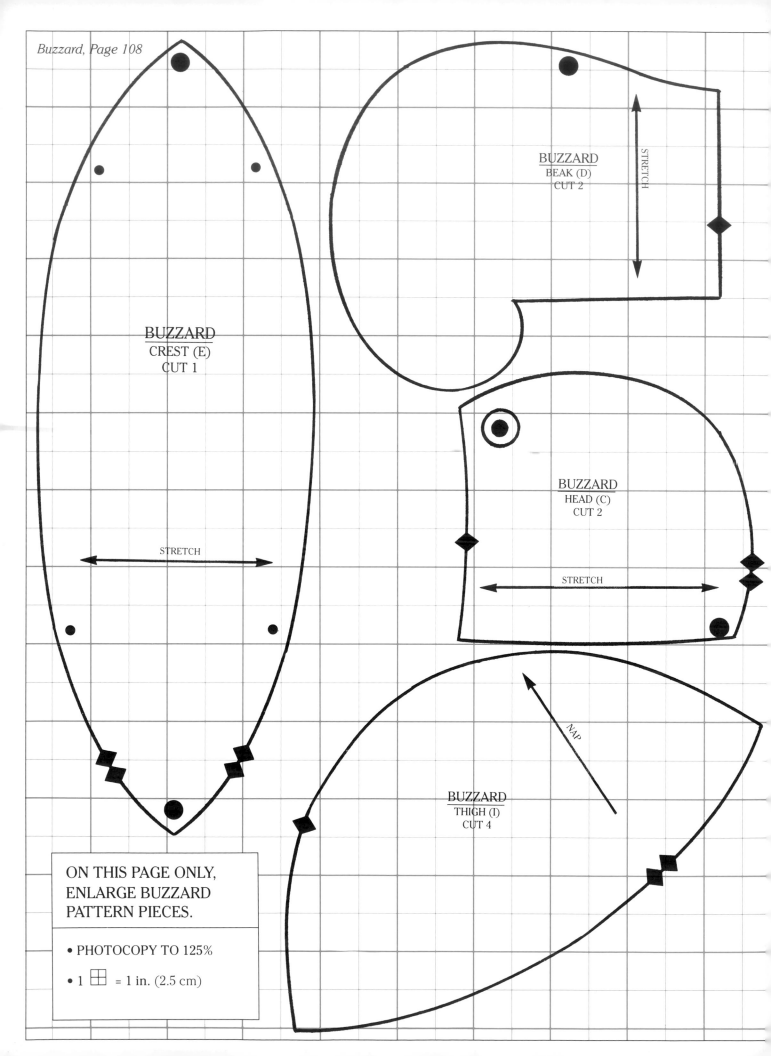

Buzzard, Page 108

BUZZARD
BEAK (D)
CUT 2

STRETCH

BUZZARD
CREST (E)
CUT 1

STRETCH

BUZZARD
HEAD (C)
CUT 2

STRETCH

NAP

BUZZARD
THIGH (I)
CUT 4

ON THIS PAGE ONLY,
ENLARGE BUZZARD
PATTERN PIECES.

• PHOTOCOPY TO 125%

• 1 ⊞ = 1 in. (2.5 cm)

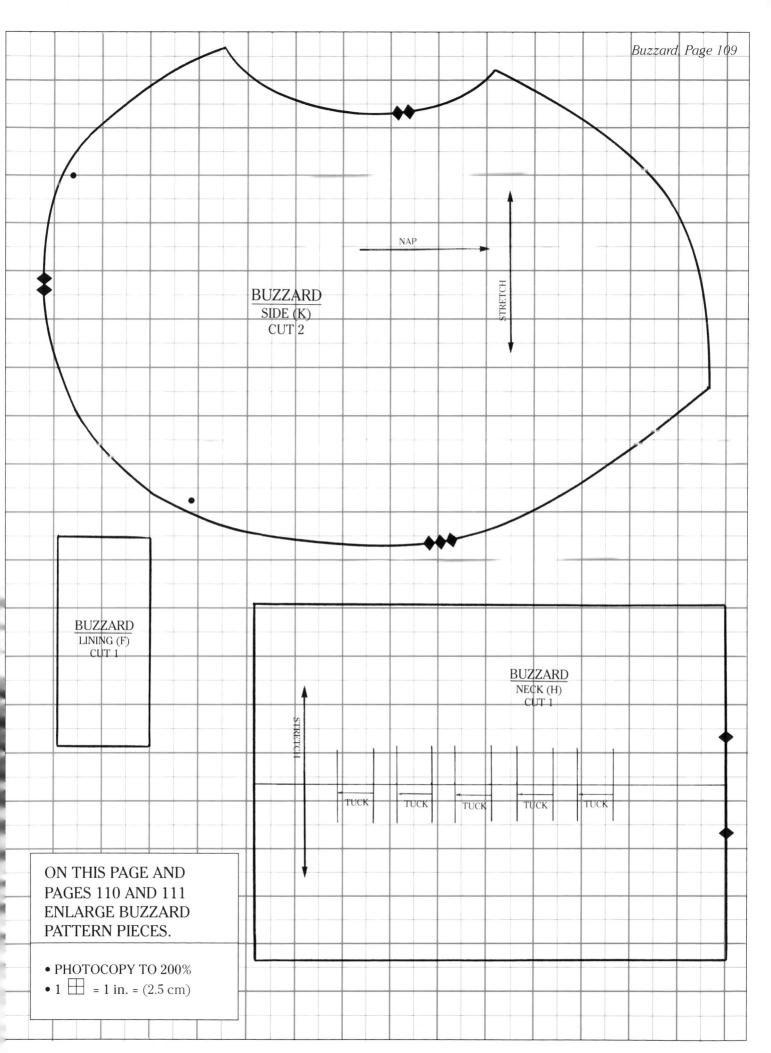

BUZZARD
SIDE (K)
CUT 2

NAP

STRETCH

BUZZARD
LINING (F)
CUT 1

BUZZARD
NECK (H)
CUT 1

STRETCH

TUCK   TUCK   TUCK   TUCK   TUCK

ON THIS PAGE AND
PAGES 110 AND 111
ENLARGE BUZZARD
PATTERN PIECES.

• PHOTOCOPY TO 200%
• 1 ⊞ = 1 in. = (2.5 cm)

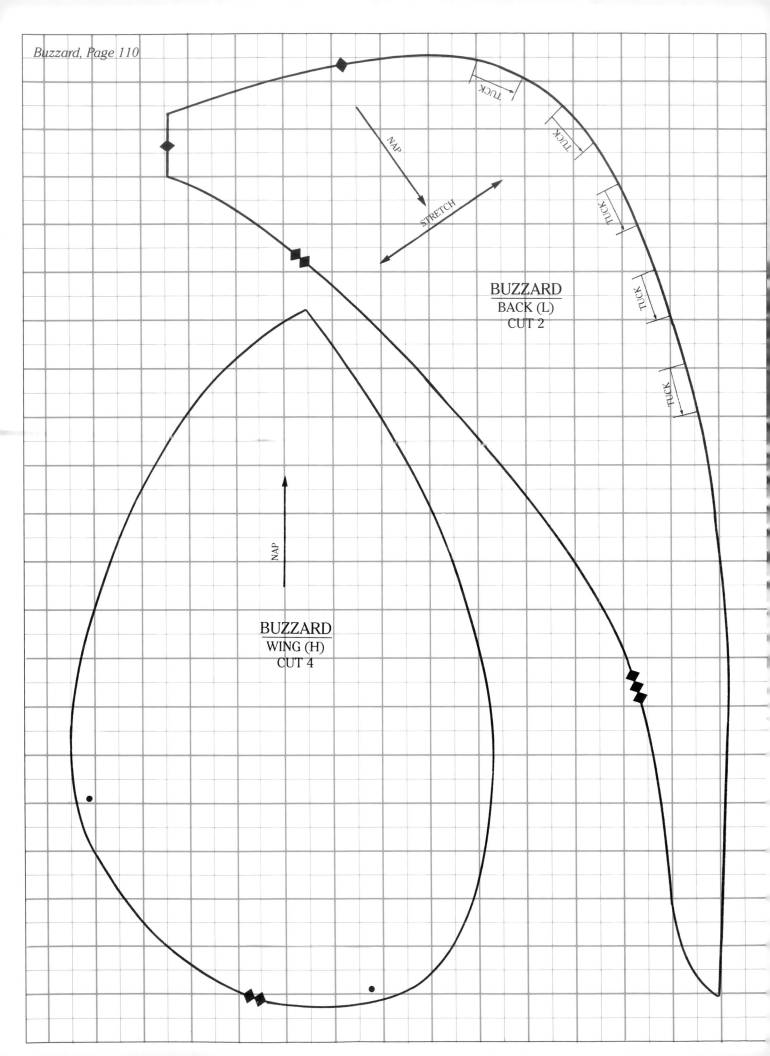

TUCK

TUCK

TUCK

TUCK

TUCK

NAP

STRETCH

BUZZARD
BACK (L)
CUT 2

NAP

BUZZARD
WING (H)
CUT 4

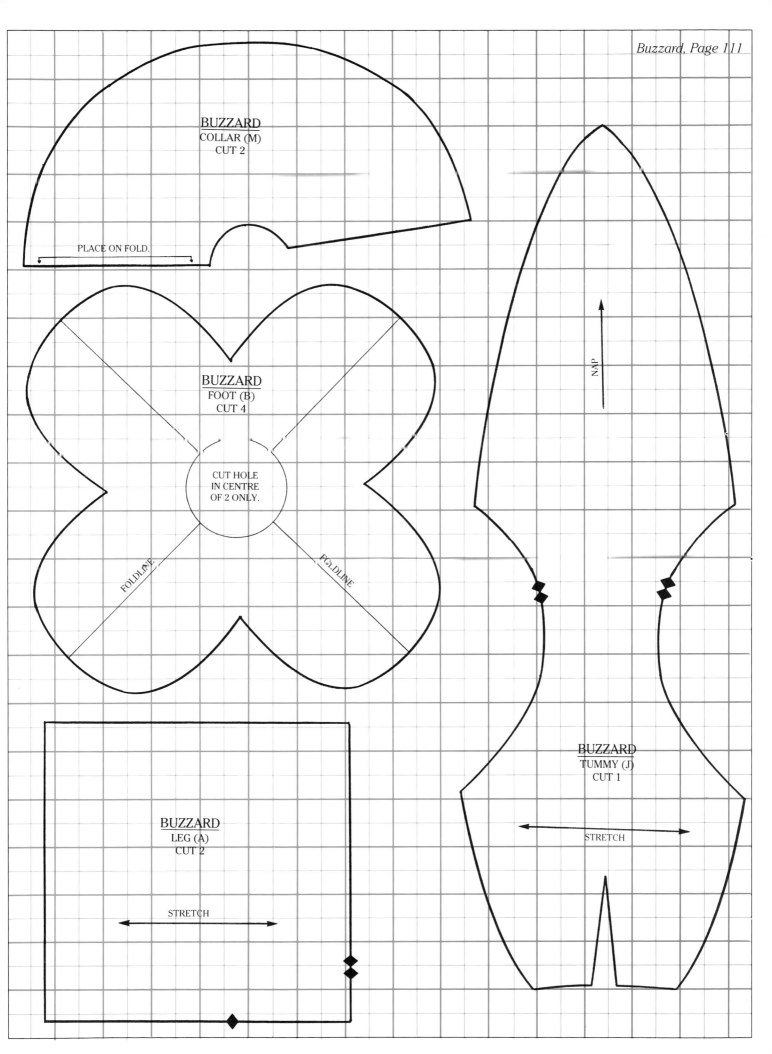

BUZZARD
COLLAR (M)
CUT 2

PLACE ON FOLD.

BUZZARD
FOOT (B)
CUT 4

CUT HOLE
IN CENTRE
OF 2 ONLY.

FOLDLINE

FOLDLINE

BUZZARD
LEG (A)
CUT 2

STRETCH

NAP

BUZZARD
TUMMY (J)
CUT 1

STRETCH

Lazy Dog

W hen a dog gives you his heart, you're his for life. However, as much attention as your dog gives you, you'll be giving him plenty more back. Here's a dog that only requires hugs. He doesn't shed and needs no walking, no feeding, no stooping-and-scooping. This quiet, maintenance-free dog lies around in that crazy way real dogs sleep, with their legs stuck out at the back.

Lazy Dog is not difficult to make. The patterns have been simplified to give the most expressive shaping with only a few pattern pieces and easy construction. Lazy Dog's paws and muzzle can be cut from white plush or plush that matches the body fur, but is sheared for a contrasting texture. (See page 13 for more information on shearing plush.)

Whether or not you make Lazy Dog to match your own Spot, Pokey or Fido, there are lots of excellent dog-like plushes available. For a touch of realism, choose doggy colors in medium-to-dark browns, tan, rust or black and white. Beware of leopard-like spots and tabby designs to avoid a doggy identity crisis. Fill Lazy Dog with extra soft filling to make him an exceptionally cuddly puppy.

Cutting

WHAT YOU NEED

Purchase plush with short, medium or long pile for the body. Use short pile for the contrasting parts.

LAZY DOG

- ½ yd. (.5 m) plush, 48 in. (120 cm) wide for body
- Remnant, 16 in. (40 cm) square plush for muzzle and paws
- Scrap, 7 in. (18 cm) square pink plush or fleece for fronts of ears

OPTIONAL

- Scrap, 4 in. (10 cm) square black velour for nose

STUFFING

- 1 lb. (500 g) synthetic filling

NOTIONS

- Two eyes (See page 22 for more information.)
- Heavy thread

CUTTING REMARKS

- Scale patterns to full size. Pin or trace them onto fabric.
- Position all pattern pieces according to cutting layout. Check whether fabric is single or double thickness and whether patterns are right or wrong side up. See "Code for Cutting and Sewing.")
- Cut accurately, directly on cutting line.
- Transfer all symbols to wrong side of fabric.
- Check for nap on pile fabrics. Position nap arrows in direction of nap.

FINISHED SIZE

← 16 in. (41 cm) →

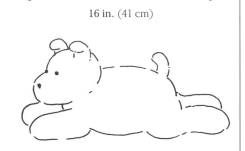

CODE FOR CUTTING AND SEWING

  Pink denotes RIGHT side of fabric.

  White denotes WRONG side of fabric.

  Yellow denotes RIGHT side of pattern.

  Dots denote WRONG side of pattern.

CUTTING LAYOUT

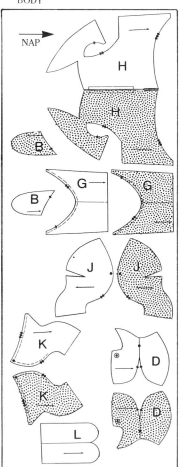

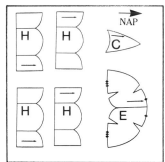

Sewing

KNOW BEFORE YOU SEW

- PINS – Use bead-headed pins for visibility and easy retrieval.
- SEAMS – Make seams 1/4 in. (.5 cm) wide.
- STITCH – Sew medium-length machine stitches.
- BASTE – Sew long machine stitches. Baste all seams before sewing.

Notch curve.   Clip curve.   Clip corner.

- NOTCH CURVE – Cut V's to seam, evenly along curve.
- CLIP CURVE – Clip to seam, evenly along inside curve.
- CLIP CORNER – Clip from inside corner to pivot in seam.
- REINFORCING – Reinforce all stress points with an extra seam.
- STUFFING – Stuff small areas firmly and larger areas less firmly.
- LADDER STITCH – Sew an invisible seam from the right side.

For more information on these or any other sewing terms, consult the glossary at the back of the book.

Head

1 Shear plush on all four ear sections unless pile is very short.

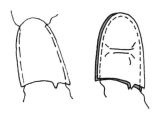

2 Sew darts in EAR-FRONT (A) sections as follows. Fold ear along center line of dart with right sides together. Sew along stitching line, as indicated on pattern.

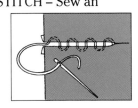

3 Ease stitch side seams of both EAR-BACK (B) sections. Gather gently. Position one ear-back section onto one ear-front section with right sides together. Stitch curved edge, adjusting ease stitching to fit. Leave end open. Notch curve.

Turn ear right-side-out. Baste end shut, close to raw edge. Repeat with remaining ear sections. Set aside.

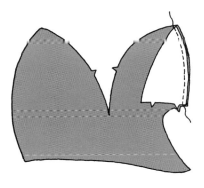

4 Position long edge of FOREHEAD (C) section on one HEAD (D) section with right sides together. Stitch. Repeat with remaining head section, so that forehead and head sections are one piece.

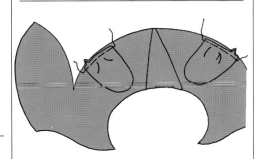

5 Lay head section flat with RIGHT SIDE UP. Position ears onto head with ear-fronts down, matching notches. Be certain short edges of ears are toward center. Baste close to raw edge.

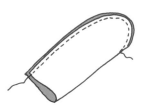

10 Fold TAIL (L) section in half lengthwise with right sides together. Stitch from fold-edge to end. Leave end open. Turn tail right-side-out. Stuff with filling. Baste open end shut. Set aside.

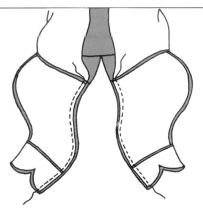

11 With dog's body wrong-side-out, flatten hind legs with right sides together. Match paw seams and place body seams on small •s. Stitch from small •s to ends of paws. DO NOT SEW ENDS OF PAWS.

12 Flatten one paw along foldlines, as indicated on pattern, with right sides together. Stitch curved edge. Notch curve. Repeat with remaining paw.

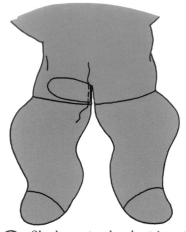

13 Slash center back at junction of hind legs 1½ in. (4 cm), as indicated on pattern.
  Lay dog body flat with RIGHT SIDE UP. Position tail with raw edge at slash of center back. Baste in place, close to raw edge.

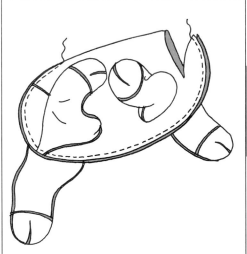

14 Fold Lazy Dog along center back with right sides together. Match seams. Beginning at center back, stitch full outside seam to end of point, sewing tail into seam. Leave seam across chest open for turning and stuffing. Notch curves.

15 Turn dog body right-side-out through chest opening. Stuff with filling.
  Using heavy thread, doubled, close opening in dog's chest with ladder stitch.

16 Position dog's head onto body, centering it on Lazy Dog's shoulders, over hand sewing. Using heavy thread, doubled, sew it securely in place with ladder stitch.

17 *Optional:* If pile is long, you may wish to shear some on face. Using small scissors, begin trimming near muzzle, working outward. Cut pile longer as you go, to blend in near ears.

18 Sit. Lay down. Roll over. Good dog, Lazy Dog, here's your cookie.

Snapshot, 1949.

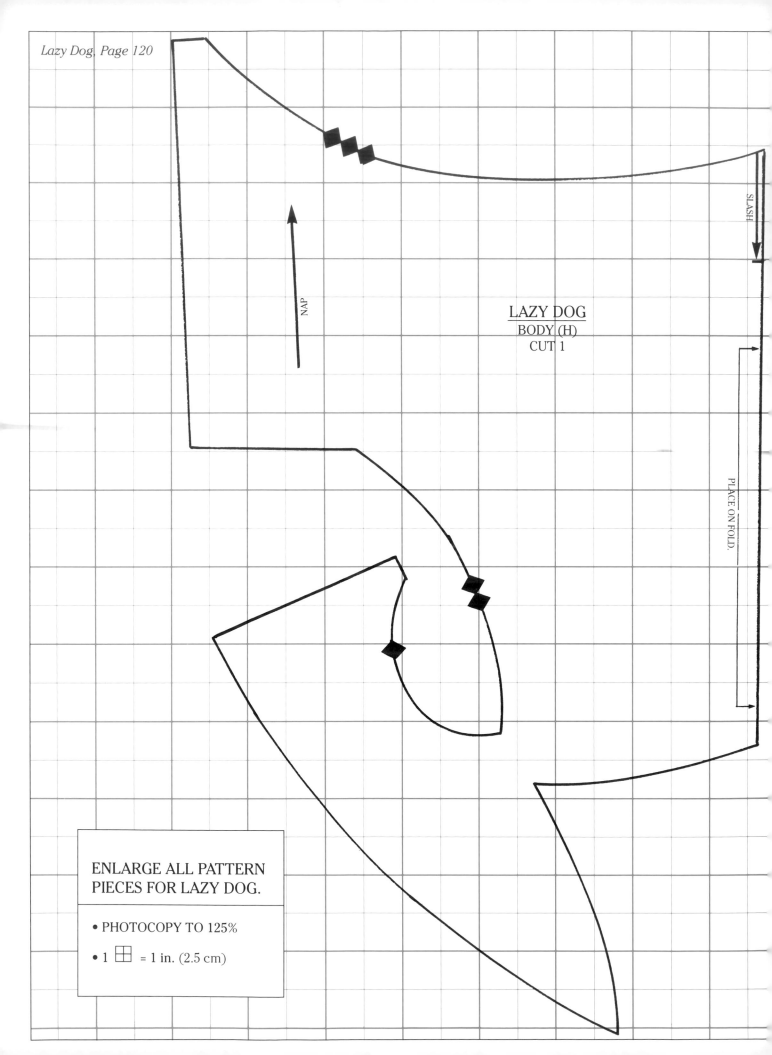

Lazy Dog, Page 120

NAP

SLASH

PLACE ON FOLD.

LAZY DOG
BODY (H)
CUT 1

ENLARGE ALL PATTERN
PIECES FOR LAZY DOG.

• PHOTOCOPY TO 125%

• 1 ⊞ = 1 in. (2.5 cm)

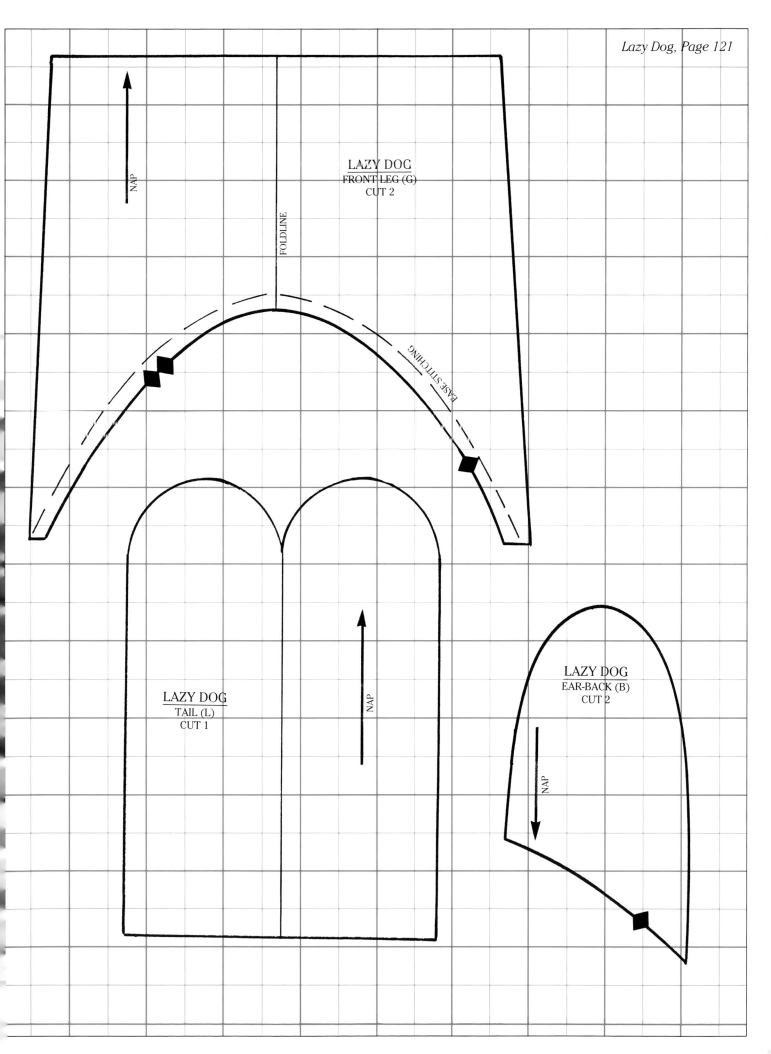

NAP

FOLDLINE

LAZY DOG
FRONT LEG (G)
CUT 2

EASE STITCHING

LAZY DOG
TAIL (L)
CUT 1

NAP

LAZY DOG
EAR-BACK (B)
CUT 2

NAP

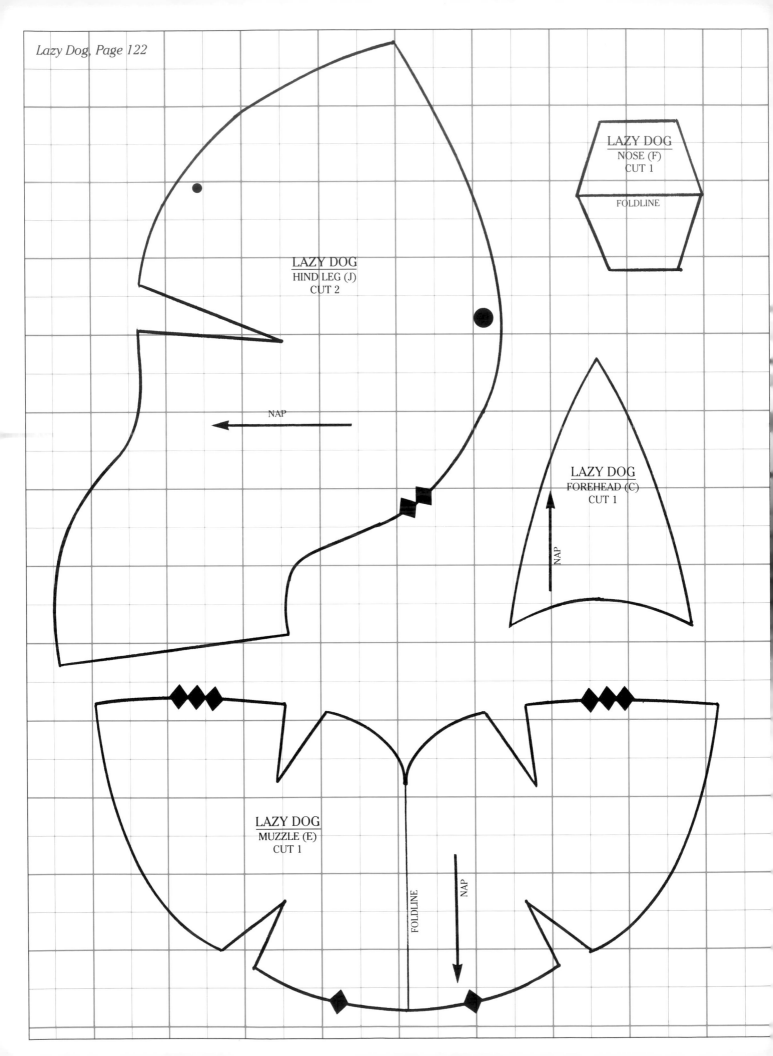

Lazy Dog, Page 122

LAZY DOG
NOSE (F)
CUT 1

FOLDLINE

LAZY DOG
HIND LEG (J)
CUT 2

NAP

LAZY DOG
FOREHEAD (C)
CUT 1

NAP

LAZY DOG
MUZZLE (E)
CUT 1

FOLDLINE

NAP

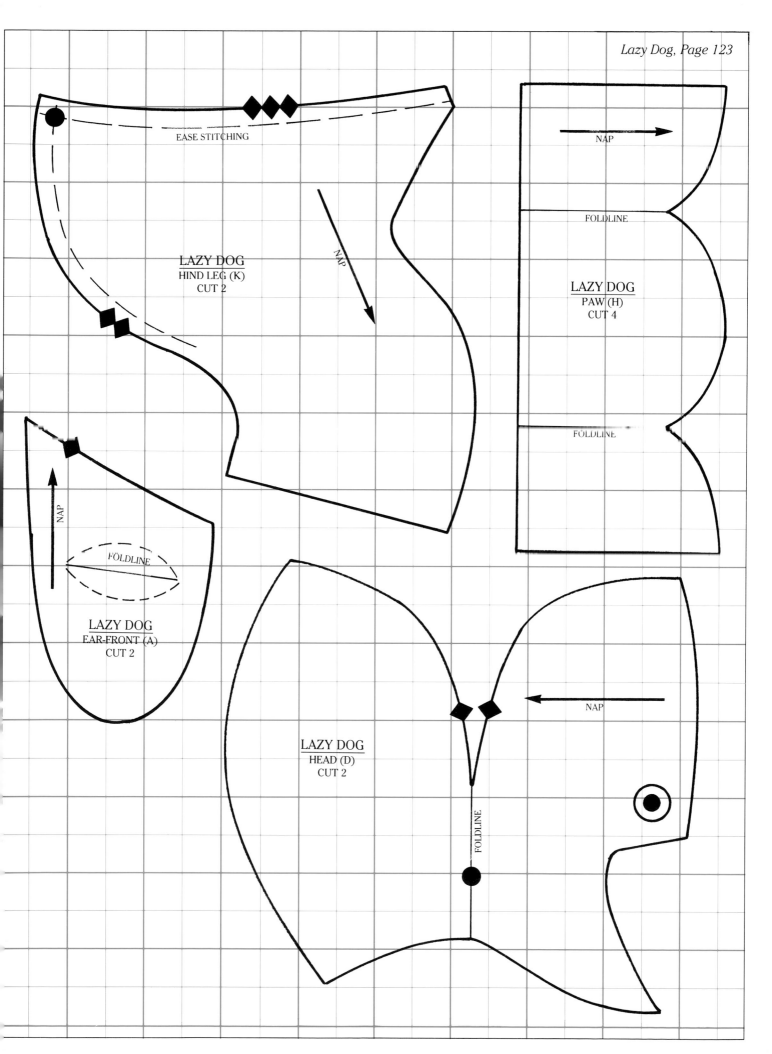

EASE STITCHING

NAP

LAZY DOG
HIND LEG (K)
CUT 2

NAP

FOLDLINE

LAZY DOG
PAW (H)
CUT 4

FOLDLINE

NAP

FÖLDLINE

LAZY DOG
EAR-FRONT (A)
CUT 2

NAP

LAZY DOG
HEAD (D)
CUT 2

FOLDLINE

Super Pig

Faster than a cheesecake, chunkier than a banana split, smaller than a meatloaf ... it's S-U-P-E-R P-I-G! By day he's a fuzzy pink-clad oinker, by night a magnificently purple-caped snacker extraordinaire. Make this surprise super-hero for adults or children. Adults love the irony. Kids love dressing and undressing the pig, when they're not helping S.P. save the population from the forces of evil.

This is a rather long project because you are, in effect, making two items. The first is the fuzzy pink pig-suit, necessary for the pig's disguise as the mild mannered pork du jour. The second is the Super Pig himself, all decked out in three-color, skin tight stretch velour complete with cape. Of course, if you wish, you can cut down on time and effort by making Super Pig without his plush pig suit.

Cutting

WHAT YOU NEED

For Piggy's tri-colored body and cape, as well as his feet, tail, ear fronts and nose, choose stretch velour or similar fabric. Avoid spandex-type fabrics that stretch in all directions. Quantities for the body are listed by color.

Choose short plush in any shade of pink for the removable suit.

SUPER PIG

- 1/2 yd. (.5 m) pink plush, 48 in. (120 cm) wide for fuzzy pink suit
- 1/4 yd. (.3 m) blue stretch velour, 40 in. (100 cm) wide
- 1/4 yd. (.3 m) red stretch velour, 36 in. (100 cm) wide
- Remnant, yellow stretch velour, 16 in. (40 cm) square
- Remnant, pink stretch velour, 24 in. (60 cm) square

STUFFING

- 1 lb. (500 g) synthetic filling

NOTIONS

- Matching thread
- 8 in. (20 cm) chunky zipper to match pink plush
- Two eyes (See page 22 for more information.)
- 4 in. (10 cm) elastic, 1/4 in. (.5 cm) wide

CUTTING REMARKS

- Scale patterns to full size. Pin or trace them onto fabric.
- Position all pattern pieces according to cutting layout. Check whether fabric is single or double thickness and whether patterns are right or wrong side up. (See "Legend for Cutting and Sewing".)
- Cut accurately, directly on cutting line.
- Transfer all symbols to wrong side of fabric.

- Cut notches outward.
- Check for nap on pile fabrics. Position nap arrows in direction of nap.
- Check stretch fabrics. Position stretch arrows in direction of stretch.

FINISHED SIZE

15 in. (38 cm)

CODE FOR CUTTING AND SEWING

Pink denotes RIGHT side of fabric.

White denotes WRONG side of fabric.

Yellow denotes RIGHT side of pattern.

Dots denote WRONG side of pattern.

CUTTING LAYOUT

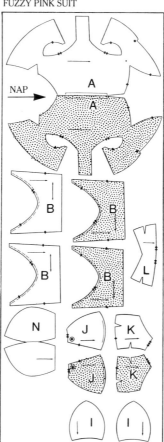

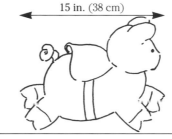

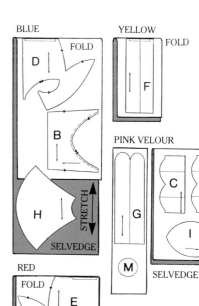

Sewing

KNOW BEFORE YOU SEW

- PINS – Use bead-headed pins for visibility and easy retrieval.
- SEAMS – Make seams ¼ in. (.5 cm) wide.
- STITCH – Sew medium-length machine stitches.
- BASTE – Sew long machine stitches. Baste all seams before sewing.

Notch curve. Clip curve. Clip corner.

- NOTCH CURVE – Cut V's to seam, evenly along curve.
- CLIP CURVE – Clip to seam, evenly along inside curve.
- CLIP CORNER – Clip from inside corner to pivot in seam.
- REINFORCING – Reinforce all stress points with an extra seam.
- STUFFING – Stuff small areas firmly and larger areas less firmly.
- LADDER STITCH – Sew an invisible seam from the right side.

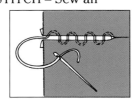

For more information on these, or any other sewing terms consult the glossary at the back of the book.

Fuzzy Pink Suit

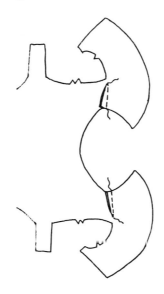

1 Stitch darts in neck edge of FUZZY PINK SUIT (A) section.

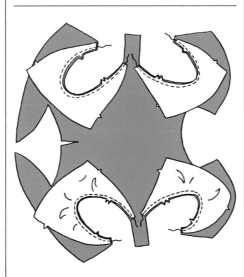

2 Ease stitch curved edge of all four fuzzy pink LEG (B) sections. Position one leg section on suit section with right sides together, matching single and double notches. Stitch full curved edge, pivoting at tight corner. Clip curve. Repeat with three remaining legs.

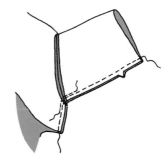

3 Fold leg in half with right sides together, matching single notches and seams. Stitch side of leg. Pivot at seam and continue to end. Reinforce corner. Repeat for three remaining legs.

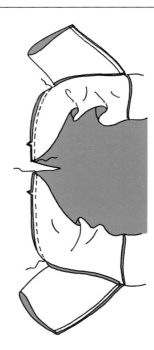

4 At rear of suit, fold V-shaped sections onto suit section, matching single notches. Starting at small •s, stitch to ends.

5 At rear of suit, fold suit in half with right sides together. Stitch from seam to large ●, leaving tail-opening open beyond seam. Notch curve.

Check whether plush frays. It shouldn't, but if it does, overcast raw edges in following steps. Turn edges of tail-opening under to wrong side. Slip stitch or machine stitch.

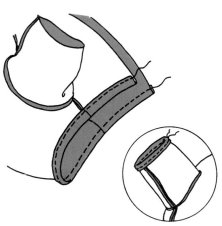

6 Turn neck edge of suit under ¼ in. (½ cm). Slip stitch or machine stitch.

Turn ends of legs under ¼ in. (½ cm) to wrong side. Slip stitch or machine stitch.

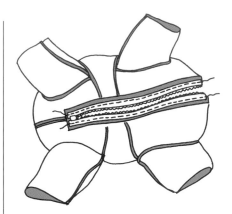

7 Beginning at large ●, turn seam under ⅝ in. (1.5 cm) on both sides of stomach seam. Hand tack.

Lay zipper open with RIGHT SIDE DOWN on WRONG SIDE of stomach seam. Baste. Stitch, using zipper foot.

Three-color Body

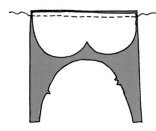

1 Position one TROTTER (C) section on one blue or red velour LEG (B) section, with right sides together. Stitch straight edge. Repeat with remaining three velour legs.

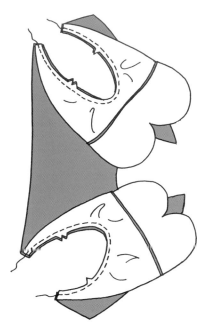

2 Position two legs on CHEST (D) section with right sides together, matching single and double notches. Be sure color matches. Stitch curved edge, pivoting at tight curve and stretching body to ease if necessary.

Repeat for remaining legs and BUM (E) section. Set bum section aside.

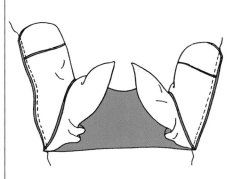

3 On chest section, fold legs in half with right sides together. Stitch straight edge of each leg. Do not sew around ends of trotters.

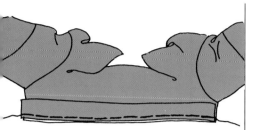

4 Fold BELT (F) section in half lengthwise with WRONG SIDES TOGETHER. Position on right side of bum section. Baste.

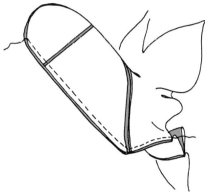

8 Fold one trotter in half with right sides together. See pattern for foldlines. Stitch ends, pivoting at seam. Trim points. Repeat for all feet.

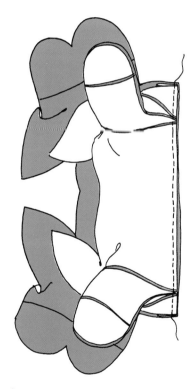

6 Fold one hind leg in half with right sides together, matching seams. Stitch side seam, pivoting at seam and continuing to end. Do not sew end of trotter. Repeat.
Note: This seam may be easier to sew in two parts.

9 Fold TAIL (G) section in half with right sides together. Baste side seam. Gather gently. Position elastic over basting. Sew, while stretching elastic. This will make the tail curly. Continue sewing around end. Turn right-side-out.

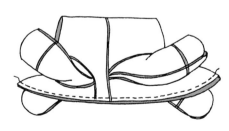

7 Lay belt flat toward bum (red) section.
Fold body in half with right sides together. Match seams and belt. Stitch full stomach edge.

5 Position chest and bum sections with right sides together. Stitch straight edge through all thicknesses, sewing belt into seam.

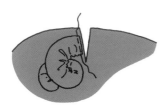

10 Slash bum section at center back, as indicated on pattern.

Position tail on RIGHT SIDE of bum section, laying raw edge of tail on slash. Baste close to raw edge. Fold bum section in half, with right sides together. Sew slash, as if sewing a dart, sewing raw edge of tail into seam.

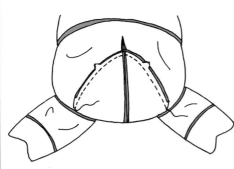

11 Position flap onto bum section with right sides together. Stitch, keeping tail free.

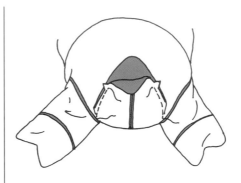

12 Position flap onto chest section with right sides together. Stitch from fold-edge to single notches. Leave open between single notches for turning and stuffing. Turn body right-side-out.

Stuff body with filling. Close chest opening with ladder stitch.

13 Turn two side edges of CAPE (H) to wrong side. Slip stitch or machine stitch. Repeat with long curved edge. Attach any appliques to right side of cape. Set aside.

Head

1 Position one fuzzy EAR (I) section onto one velour ear section with right sides together. Stitch curved edge. Turn right-side-out.

Top stitch $1/2$ in. (1 cm) from edge Repeat with remaining ear section.

2 Position two FACE-FRONT (J) sections with right sides together. Stitch unnotched center seam.

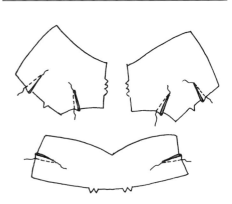

3 Stitch darts in FACE-SIDE (K) sections. Stitch darts in SNOUT (L) section.

4 Position face-side on face-front, matching single notch. Stitch single-notched edge. Repeat so that face-front and face-side sections are all one piece.

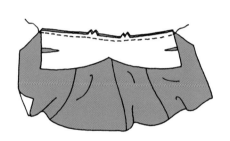

5 Position snout section on face section with right sides together, matching double notches. Stitch double-notched edge.

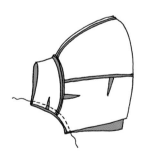

6 Fold face in half with right sides together, matching seams. Stitch snout-chin seam.

7 Position NOSE (M) section into open end of snout with right sides together.
Note: Place presser foot INSIDE snout for easier sewing.

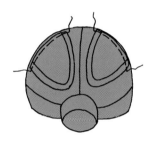

8 Position ears onto RIGHT SIDE of face with velour down. See pattern for placement. Baste close to raw edge.

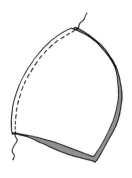

9 Fold HEAD (N) in half with right sides together. Stitch center seam.

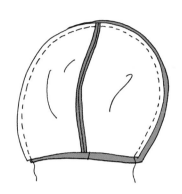

10 Position head on face-front with right sides together. Stitch curved edge. Leave straight edge open for turning and stuffing. Turn right-side-out.

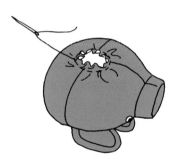

11 Attach eyes. See pattern for placement. (See page 22 for more information.)
Hand baste neck edge. Stuff head with filling. Draw up basting. Tie off.

12 Put body into fuzzy pink suit and close zipper. The neck opening of suit indicates placement of cape and head. Position cape under head. Hand tack without catching pink suit in stitching.

Position head at neck opening of suit. Hand tack or mark and remove pink suit. Ladder stitch head securely in place.

13 Super Pig says, it's time for a break.

Snapshot 1955

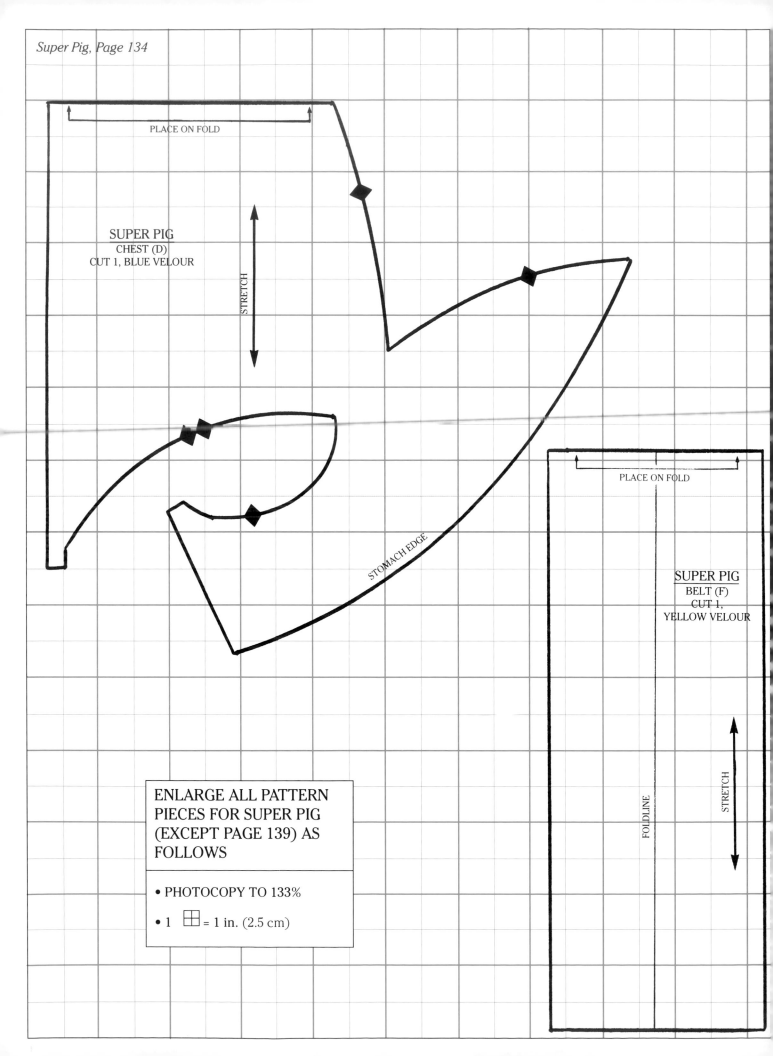

Super Pig, Page 134

PLACE ON FOLD

SUPER PIG
CHEST (D)
CUT 1, BLUE VELOUR

STRETCH

STOMACH EDGE

PLACE ON FOLD

SUPER PIG
BELT (F)
CUT 1,
YELLOW VELOUR

FOLDLINE

STRETCH

ENLARGE ALL PATTERN
PIECES FOR SUPER PIG
(EXCEPT PAGE 139) AS
FOLLOWS

• PHOTOCOPY TO 133%

• 1 ⊞ = 1 in. (2.5 cm)

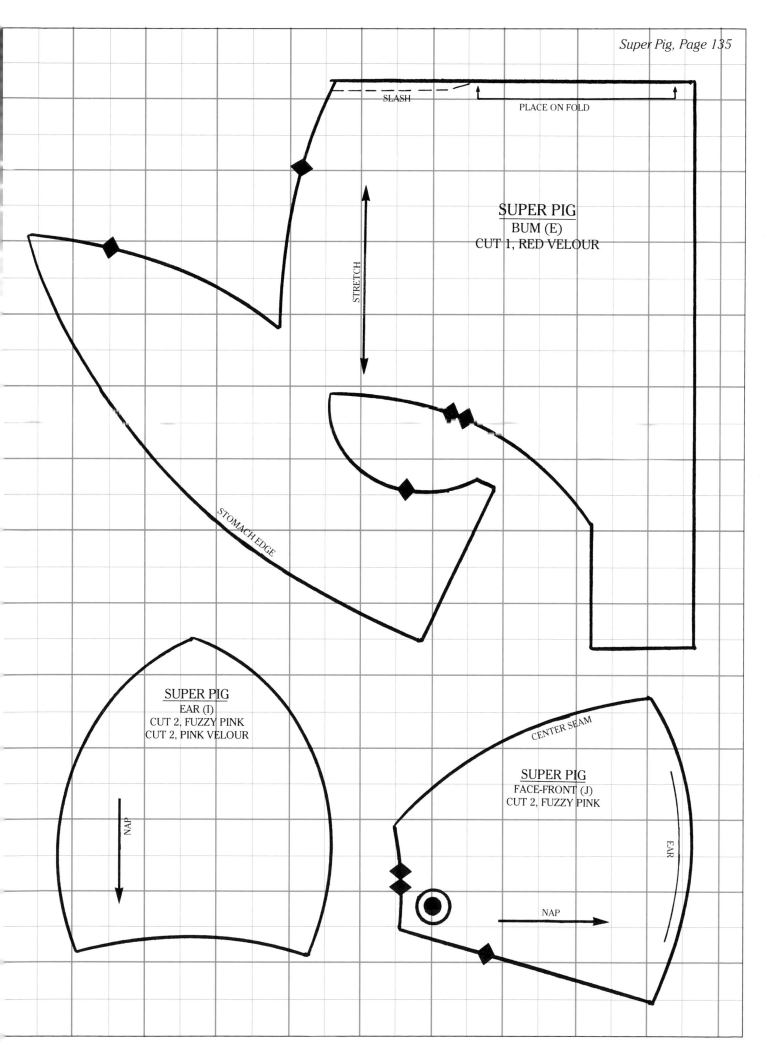

SLASH

PLACE ON FOLD

SUPER PIG
BUM (E)
CUT 1, RED VELOUR

STRETCH

STOMACH EDGE

SUPER PIG
EAR (I)
CUT 2, FUZZY PINK
CUT 2, PINK VELOUR

NAP

CENTER SEAM

SUPER PIG
FACE-FRONT (J)
CUT 2, FUZZY PINK

EAR

NAP

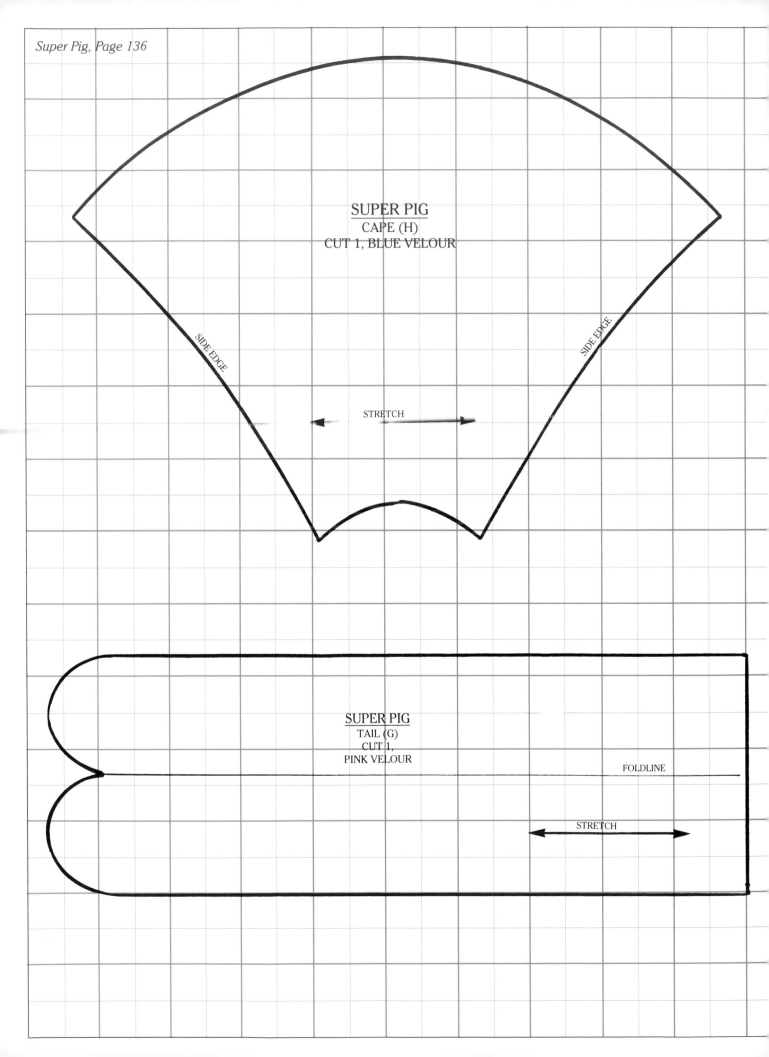

SUPER PIG
CAPE (H)
CUT 1, BLUE VELOUR

SIDE EDGE

SIDE EDGE

STRETCH

SUPER PIG
TAIL (G)
CUT 1,
PINK VELOUR

FOLDLINE

STRETCH

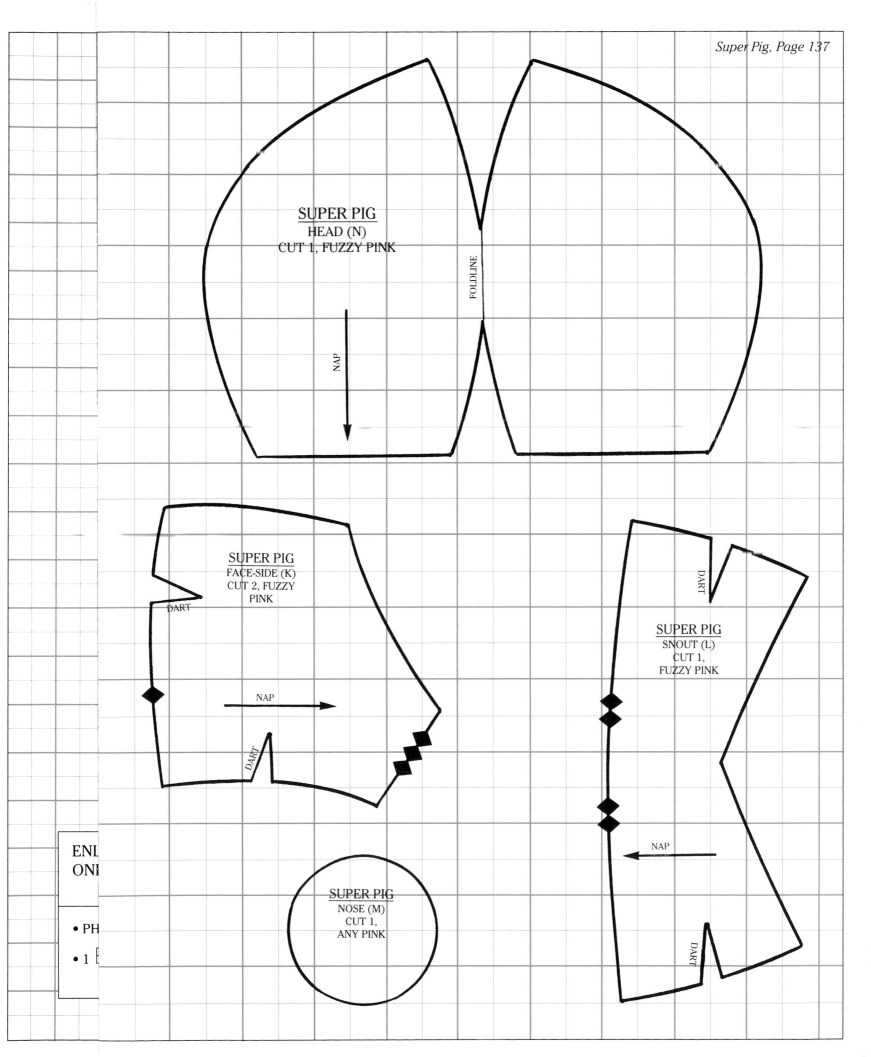

SUPER PIG
HEAD (N)
CUT 1, FUZZY PINK

FOLDLINE

NAP

SUPER PIG
FACE-SIDE (K)
CUT 2, FUZZY
PINK

DART

DART

NAP

SUPER PIG
SNOUT (L)
CUT 1,
FUZZY PINK

DART

NAP

DART

SUPER PIG
NOSE (M)
CUT 1,
ANY PINK

ENL
ONI

• PH

• 1

Firefly

W hat would summer be without everyone's favorite bug, the firefly? Here's a glowing reminder of warm summer nights in the form of a friendly, fun handpuppet. Wear the firefly like a glove with your fingers in five of the six legs. Then fly her around, land, and creep up the neck of an unsuspecting, snoozing TV watcher.

The richness of the black stretch velour for the body and legs is a wonderful contrast for the glowing, neon nylon bum and the crispy-looking iridescent wings.

Cut more than one to make a whole swarm.

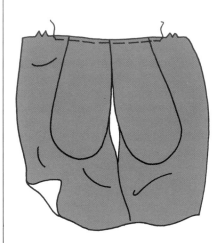

3 Lay back section flat with RIGHT SIDE UP. Position raw edge of wings on notched edge of back, on either side of center seam. Baste close to raw edge.

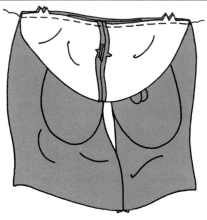

4 Position head section on back section with right sides together, matching center seams and double notches. Stitch seam, stretching body gently to fit. Sew wings into seam, keeping antennae free.

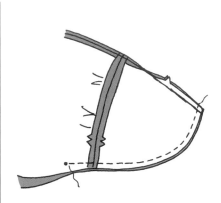

5 Fold head in half with right sides together, matching neck seams. Sew curve from small • on body, along curve on head, to end. Clip seam at small •. Turn right-side-out.

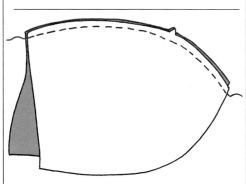

6 Position BUM (E) sections with right sides together, matching single notches. Stitch center single-notched seam.

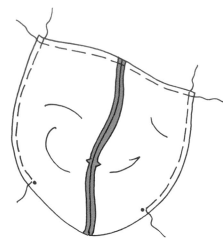

7 Open out bum section. Baste straight edge, close to raw edge. Baste curved edge, close to raw edge, between large ●s and straight edges.

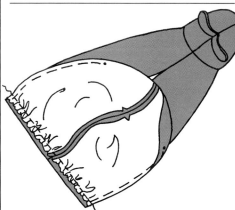

8 Gather straight edge of bum section. Position gathered edge of bum on straight edge of body with right sides together. Match center seams. DO NOT STRETCH VELOUR. Adjust gathers to fit. Stitch.

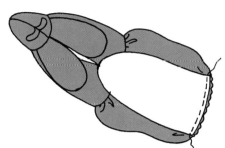

9 Position straight edge of TUMMY (F) section onto curved edge of bum section with right sides together. Stretch tummy section to fit between large ●s on bum section. Pin. Stitch, while stretching tummy section. Set aside.

Glove

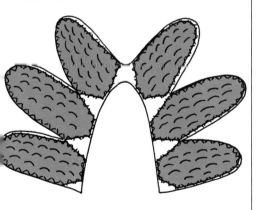

1 With WRONG SIDES TOGETHER, position quilt LEGS (G) section onto velour LEGS (G) section. Pin.

Cut out triangles ON QUILT ONLY, as marked on pattern. Using thread to match velour, stitch full edge of quilt, close to quilt edge. Use zigzag or straight stitch.

In following steps, quilt side is the wrong side.

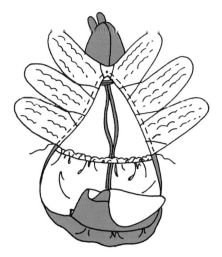

2 Position quilted legs section onto body with right sides together. Place small ● on seam. Adjust and pin. Legs should end at center-body seam. Stitch.

3 Gather remaining basting on bum section.

With WRONG SIDES TOGETHER, position curved edge of stomach section onto inside of body. Starting at small ● at head end, pin along each side. Adjust gathers. Baste, then stitch.

This may seem strange, but it is correct.

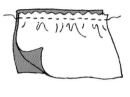

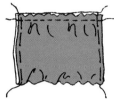

4 Position long edges of neon WRIST (H) and velour WRIST (I) sections with right sides together. Stretch velour to fit neon and stitch one long edge. Turn right-side-out.

With WRONG SIDES TOGETHER, repeat, stretching velour to fit. Baste sides.

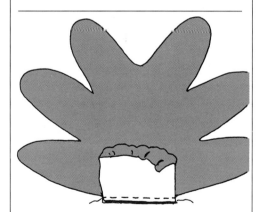

5 Position NEON side of the wrist section onto RIGHT SIDE of GLOVE (J) section. Raw edge of wrist should be on straight edge of glove section. Stitch.

6 Fold the head, wings and body into center. Pin in place, away from legs. Pin on wrong side for easy visibility and easy retrieval of pins.

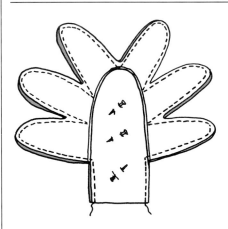

7 Position glove section onto legs and body with right sides together. WITH BODY SIDE UP, stitch full outer-edge seam, sewing around fingers and pivoting between fingers at seam in body. Leave end of wrist open.

8 Notch curves and clip corners if necessary. Turn Firefly right-side-out. Stuff the head, body and bum with filling

Using ladder stitch, close opening in Firefly's back.

9 Fold face along foldlines and match small •s, as marked on pattern. Slip stitch mouth.

Create eyes with French knots, using three strands of six-strand embroidery thread. (See page 22 or 24 for more information.)

Snapshot 1932

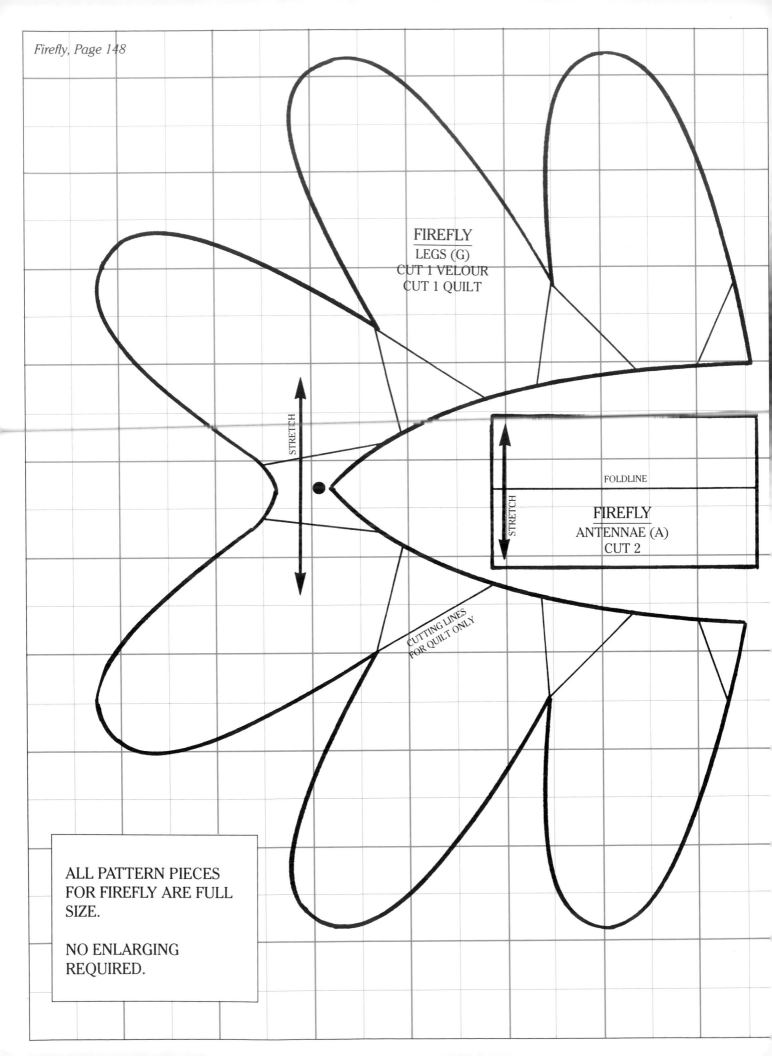

Firefly, Page 148

FIREFLY

LEGS (G)

CUT 1 VELOUR

CUT 1 QUILT

STRETCH

FOLDLINE

STRETCH

FIREFLY

ANTENNAE (A)

CUT 2

CUTTING LINES
FOR QUILT ONLY

ALL PATTERN PIECES
FOR FIREFLY ARE FULL
SIZE.

NO ENLARGING
REQUIRED.

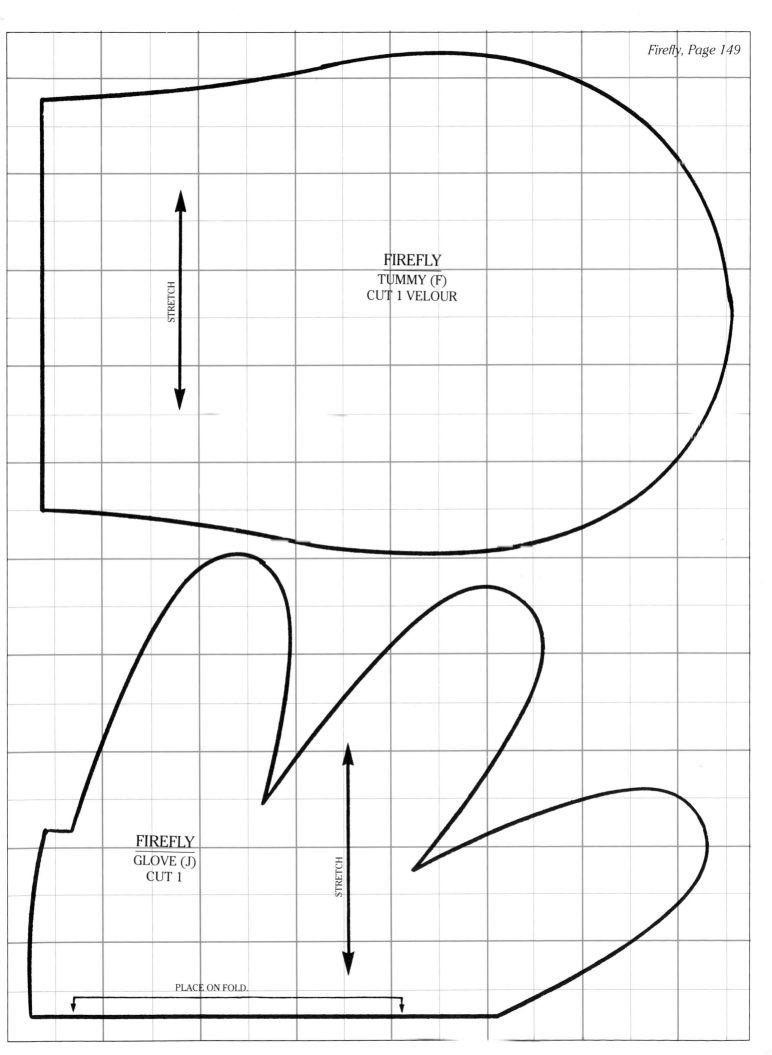

STRETCH

FIREFLY
TUMMY (F)
CUT 1 VELOUR

FIREFLY
GLOVE (J)
CUT 1

STRETCH

PLACE ON FOLD.

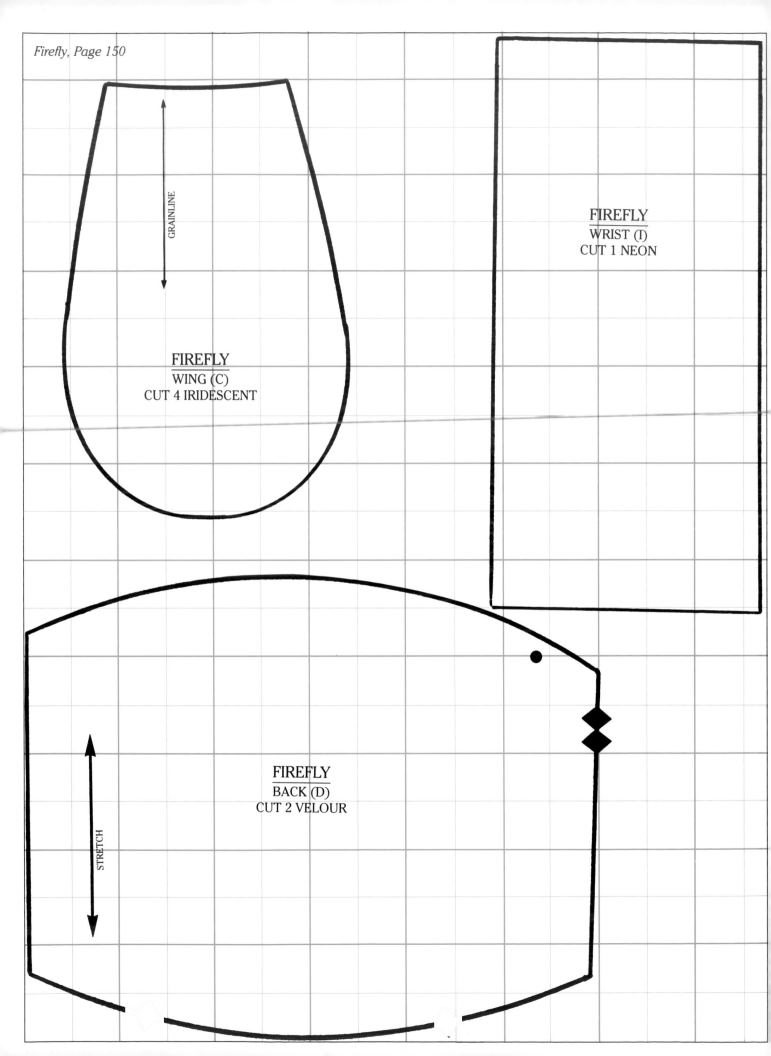

Firefly, Page 150

FIREFLY
WRIST (I)
CUT 1 NEON

GRAINLINE

FIREFLY
WING (C)
CUT 4 IRIDESCENT

FIREFLY
BACK (D)
CUT 2 VELOUR

STRETCH

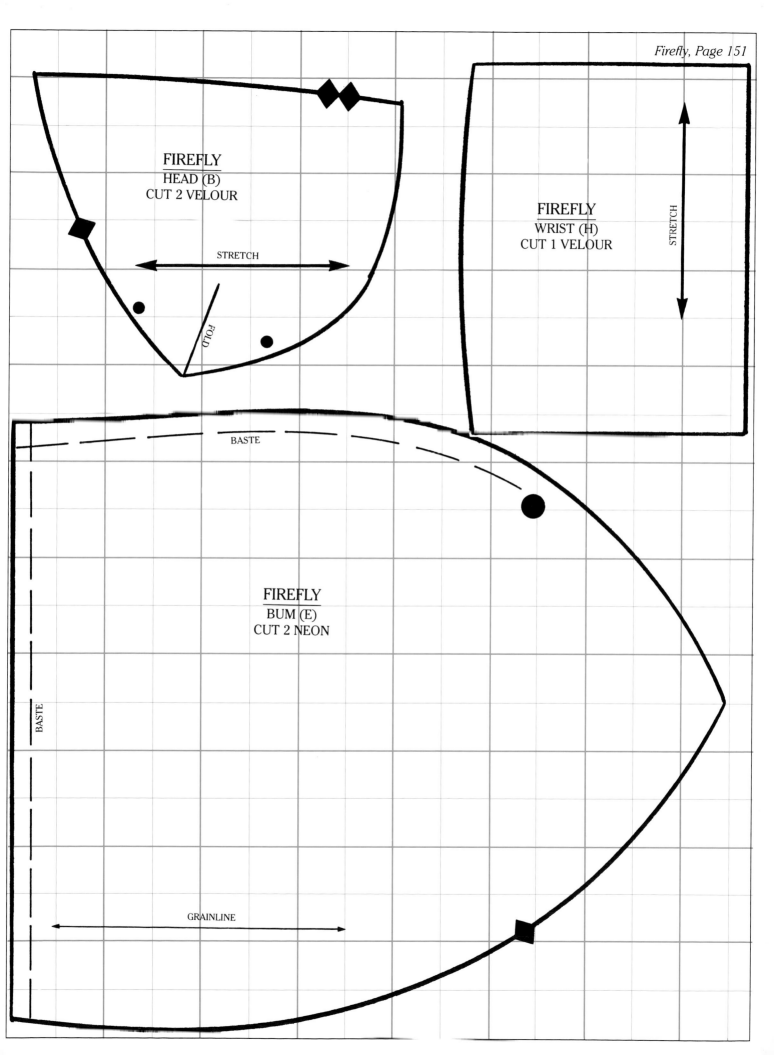

FIREFLY
HEAD (B)
CUT 2 VELOUR

STRETCH

FOLD

FIREFLY
WRIST (H)
CUT 1 VELOUR

STRETCH

BASTE

FIREFLY
BUM (E)
CUT 2 NEON

BASTE

GRAINLINE

Crocodile

P eter of the jungle thrashes his way out of the tsetse fly infested swamp with his catch — a giant, neon crocodile. But is this crocodile with his lazy eyes, zipper-toothed smile and large dimensions a sculpture, a toy or a pillow? However you use this humorously savage and decorative beast, it works beautifully.

I've made Croc with neon, textured nylon which is washable and has the interesting properties of being both crunchy and very soft. However, if you create Croc as a sculpture, try glowing, opulent silk for instant sophistication and luxury. Croc's large size is impressive, and the scrunchy texture that you get from all the sewn-in elastic is extremely touchable.

There is a lot of sewing in this crocodile, with elastic sewn into most seams and the rest gathered. Choose multi-colors carefully. Think tropical beaches, palm trees and azure seas. Then add the unexpected: a print, a fluorescent or neon, for the nostrils, lips, back bumps or eyelids. Every crocodile needs the catch of the day, so make Croc a little fish to keep him happy.

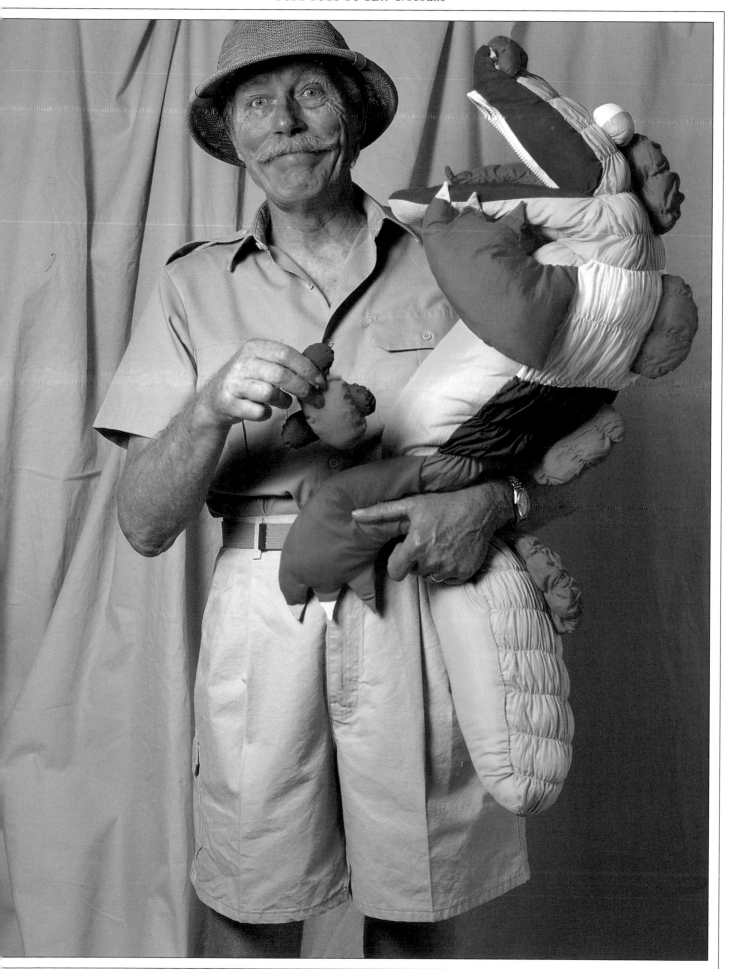

Cutting

WHAT YOU NEED

Purchase wovens that fray very little. Textured light-weight nylon which comes in a wide variety of vivid colors is excellent. For opulence, try raw silk, silky synthetics or rayon. If wovens fray easily, overcast edges before sewing. Fabric quantities are specified by color. Check photo on previous page for color references. Other colors can be substituted.

CROC

- ³/₄ yd. (.8 m) green, 36 in. (100 cm) wide
- ¹/₂ yd. (.5 m) pink, 36 in. (100 cm) wide
- ¹/₄ yd. (.3 m) orange, 36 in. (100 cm) wide
- 3 remnants, yellow, blue and red, each 12 x 24 in. (20 x 60 cm)
- Scrap, white, 10 in. (25 cm) square

STUFFING

- 1 ¹/₂ lb. (750 g) synthetic filling

NOTIONS

- Black embroidery thread
- Matching thread for top stitching
- 19 in. (48 cm) chunky, separating, white zipper

LITTLE FISH

- Scrap, 8 in. (20 cm) square for body
- Use leftover scraps, stuffing and thread from Croc for fins and tail.

CUTTING REMARKS

- Scale patterns to full size. Pin or trace them onto fabric.
- Position all pattern pieces according to cutting layout. Check whether fabric is single or double thickness and whether patterns are right or wrong side up. (See "Code for Cutting and Sewing".)
- Cut accurately, directly on cutting line.

- Transfer all symbols to wrong side of fabric.
- Cut notches outward.
- Check wovens for grain. Position grainline arrows in direction of grain.

FINISHED SIZE

44 in. (110 cm)

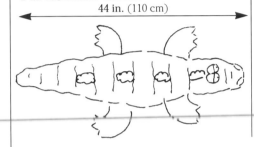

CODE FOR CUTTING AND SEWING

 Pink denotes RIGHT side of fabric.

 White denotes WRONG side of fabric.

 Yellow denotes RIGHT side of pattern.

 Dots denote WRONG side of pattern.

CUTTING LAYOUT

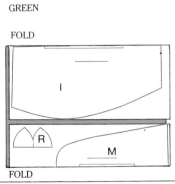

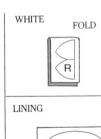

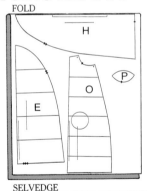

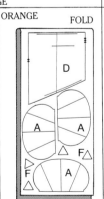

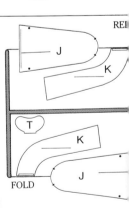

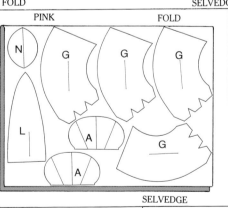

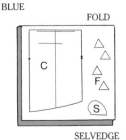

Sewing

KNOW BEFORE YOU SEW

- **PINS** – Use bead-headed pins for visibility and easy retrieval.
- **SEAMS** – Make seams 1/4 in. (.5 cm) wide.
- **STITCH** – Sew medium-length machine stitches.
- **BASTE** – Sew long machine stitches. Baste all seams before sewing.

Notch curve. Clip curve. Clip corner.

- **NOTCH CURVE** – Cut V's to seam, evenly along curve.
- **CLIP CURVE** – Clip to seam, evenly along inside curve.
- **CLIP CORNER** – Clip from inside corner to pivot in seam.
- **REINFORCING** – Reinforce all stress points with an extra seam.
- **STUFFING** – Stuff small areas firmly and larger areas less firmly.
- **LADDER STITCH** – Sew an invisible seam from the right side.

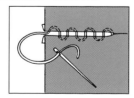

For more information on these or any other sewing terms, consult the glossary at the back of the book.

Bumps

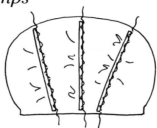

1 On WRONG SIDE of one BACK-BUMPS (A) section, stretch and sew elastic on three lines, as marked on pattern. Repeat for all remaining back-bumps sections.

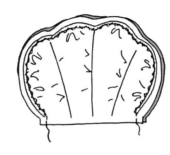

2 Position two back-bumps sections with right sides together. Baste curved edge. Stretch and sew elastic on seamline of curved edge. Leave straight edge open for turning and stuffing. Clip corners. Repeat for all back-bumps sections.

3 Turn back-bumps sections right-side-out. Stuff with filling. Baste straight edge shut, close to raw edge. Set aside. Repeat for all back-bumps.

Back

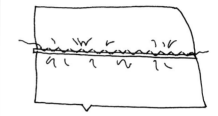

1 On the wrong side of all BACK (B), (C) and (D) sections (six sections in total), stretch and sew elastic on lines marked on pattern.

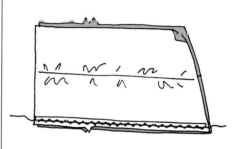

2 Position one BACK (B) section on one BACK (C) section with right sides together, matching single notches. Stretch and sew elastic on seamline.

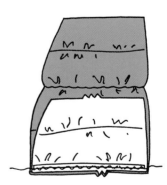

3 Position one BACK (D) section on BACK (C) section with right sides together, matching double notches. Stretch and sew elastic on seamline. Repeat steps 2 and 3 with remaining back sections.

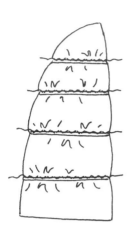

4 On wrong side of one UPPER-TAIL (E) section, stretch and sew elastic on lines, as marked on pattern. Repeat with remaining tail section.

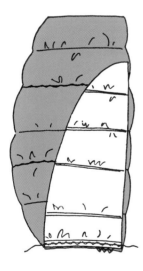

5 Position edge of UPPER TAIL (E) section onto BACK (D) (orange) section with right sides together, matching triple notches. Stretch and sew elastic on seamline. Repeat. You should now have two back-and-tail sections.

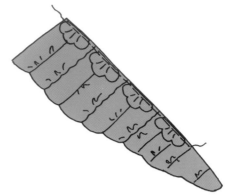

6 Lay one back-and-tail section flat, RIGHT SIDE UP. Position four back-bumps sections on center seam. See pattern for placement. Baste close to raw edge. There will be one back-bump left. Set it aside.

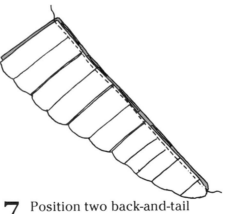

7 Position two back-and-tail sections with right sides together. Stitch center seam, sewing back bumps into seam. Do not sew elastic into seam.

Legs

1 Position two TOENAIL (F) sections with right sides together. Stitch two sides. Trim point. Turn right-side-out. Repeat for all toenails.

2 Position the raw edges of three toenails on RIGHT SIDE of one LEG (G) section at ends of toes. Baste close to raw edge. Repeat with remaining three legs and toenails.

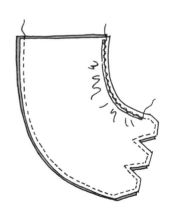

3 Position two leg sections with right sides together. Stretch and sew elastic onto INSIDE curved edge only. Continue sewing around toes, pivoting at corners and sewing toenails into seam. Continue sewing remaining curved edge. Leave straight end open for turning and stuffing. Clip corners and notch curve. Repeat with remaining six leg sections.

4 Turn one leg right-side-out. Stuff with filling. Baste open end shut, close to raw edge. Repeat with remaining three legs.

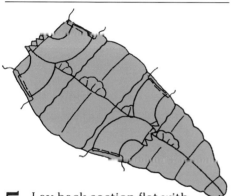

5 Lay back section flat with RIGHT SIDE UP. Position legs on right side of back section. See pattern for placement. Baste close to raw edge.

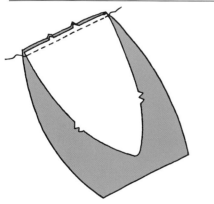

6 Position LOWER-TAIL (H) section on STOMACH (I) section, with right sides together, matching single notches. Stitch single-notched edge.

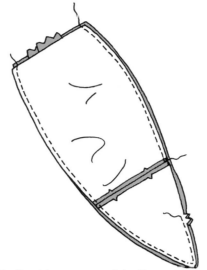

7 Position stomach/tail section on back section with right sides together, matching seams and double notches. Stitch from seam to end on one side. Then stitch from double notch, around end of tail and sew full edge. Leave area open between seam and double notches for turning and stuffing. Leave end open to attach head. Set aside.

Head

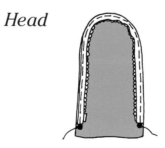

1 Position half of zipper on right side of one MOUTH (J) section between large ●s. Baste close to edge.

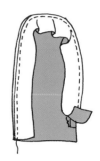

2 Position one LIPS (K) section on mouth-zipper section with right sides together. Baste, then stitch using a zipper foot.

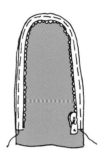

3 Repeat steps 1 and 2 with other half of zipper, mouth and lip sections, checking that zipper closings correspond.

4 Position two TONGUE (L) sections with right sides together. Stretch and sew elastic on side seams. Stitch point, without elastic. Leave end open for turning and stuffing. Trim point.
~~Turn right-side-out. Stuff with filling.~~ Baste open end shut near raw edge.

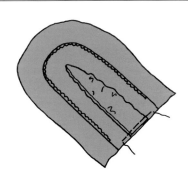

5 Position tongue on RIGHT SIDE of one mouth section. See pattern for placement. Baste close to raw edge.

6 Position two mouth sections with right sides together. Close zipper. Stitch straight edge.

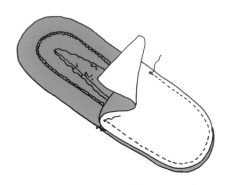

7 Open zipper and lay mouth open flat with RIGHT SIDE UP. Position BOTTOM JAW (M) section onto mouth with right sides together, placing small •s at seams. Stitch between small •s. Set aside.

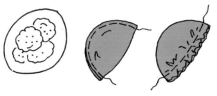

8 With one NOSTRIL (N) section WRONG SIDE UP, place a wad of filling in the center. Fold nostril in half with WRONG SIDES TOGETHER along foldline, as indicated on pattern. Baste curved edge.
   Gather curved edge so that it is almost straight. Repeat with remaining nostril.

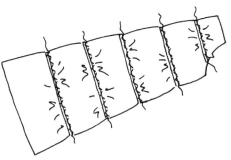

9 On wrong side of one HEAD (O) section, stretch and sew elastic along lines, as marked on pattern. Repeat with remaining head section.

10 Position nostril on RIGHT SIDE of one head section between small •s. Baste close to raw edge. Repeat with remaining nostril and head sections.

11 Position one SNOUT (P) section onto nostril with right sides together, matching single notches. Stitch. Repeat with remaining snout and head sections.

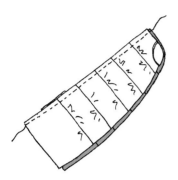

12 Position last back-bump onto one head section. See pattern for placement. Baste.
Position two head sections with right sides together. Stitch center seam, sewing back-bump into seam. Be sure to keep nostrils free.

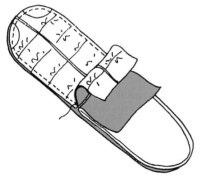

13 Lay mouth open flat with RIGHT SIDE UP. Position head section onto remaining half of mouth section with right sides together, placing small •s on seam. Stitch between small •s, keeping nostrils free.

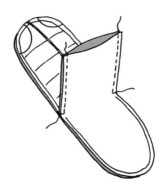

14 Position loose ends of head and bottom jaw sections with right sides together. Stitch from small •s to ends. Turn right-side-out.

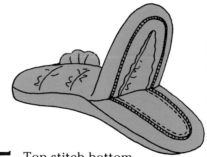

15 Top stitch bottom jaw ¹/₄ in. (.5 cm) from inside edge of zipper, through all thicknesses. Do not sew tape-edge of zipper or teeth of zipper into top stitching. End top stitching at center seam of mouth.

16 Lay head section flat with zipper closed and top-side-up. Fold back open edge to expose mouth construction. Stitch mouth to bottom jaw between seams.

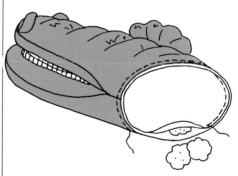

17 Position LINING (Q) section into open end of head, placing small •s on side seams. Baste close to raw edge, leaving an opening approximately 6 in. (15 cm) for stuffing.
Stuff Crocodile's head with filling. Baste opening shut.

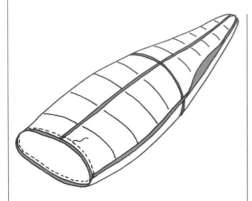

18 Turn body WRONG-SIDE-OUT. Baste around open end, close to raw edge. Gather gently.

Position head inside body. They will be right sides together. Match side seams and center-top seam. Adjust gathers. Stitch around end. Reinforce with second seam.

19 Turn Croc right-side-out through opening in tail. Stuff body with filling. Use ladder stitch to close tail opening.

Eyes

1 Fold one EYE (R) section in half with right sides together. Stitch center seam including fold edge. Repeat for remaining three eye sections.

2 Position one white and one green eye section with right sides together, matching seams. Stitch center seam. Repeat with remaining eye sections.

3 Baste raw edge of one eye section. Gather gently and stuff firmly. Then gather tightly and tie off. Repeat with remaining eye.

4 Position and stitch in place with ladder stitch. See pattern for placement.

Sew black dots on crocodile's eye with embroidery thread. Use satin stitch.

Little Fish

1 Position two FIN (S) sections right sides together. Baste curved edge. Gather. Stay stitch gathers with small stitches. Repeat with remaining two fin sections.

Repeat with two TAIL (T) sections.

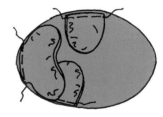

2 Position fins and tail on the RIGHT SIDE of one BODY (U) section. See pattern for placement. Baste close to raw edge.

3 Position two body sections with right sides together. Baste edge, stopping at notches. Gather. Stay stitch gathers with small stitches. Turn body right-side-out.

4 Stuff fish with filling. Using ladder stitch, close opening in body.

Birthday party photo, 1950

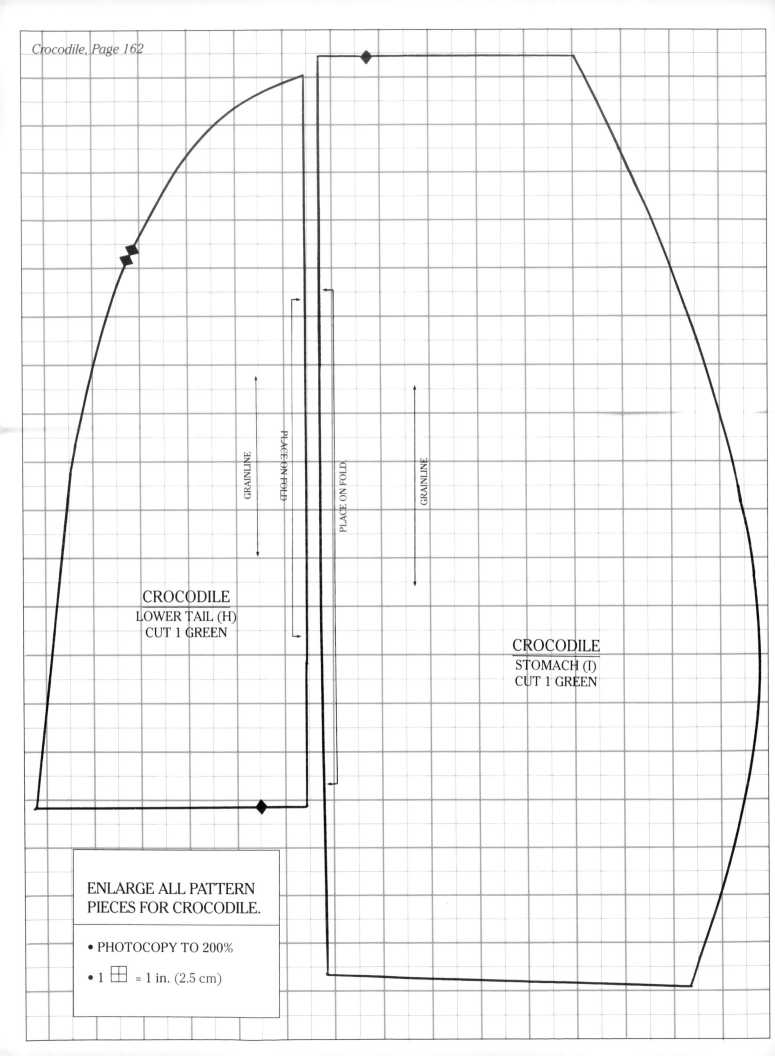

GRAINLINE

PLACE ON FOLD

PLACE ON FOLD.

GRAINLINE

CROCODILE
LOWER TAIL (H)
CUT 1 GREEN

CROCODILE
STOMACH (I)
CUT 1 GREEN

ENLARGE ALL PATTERN
PIECES FOR CROCODILE.

• PHOTOCOPY TO 200%

• 1 ⊞ = 1 in. (2.5 cm)

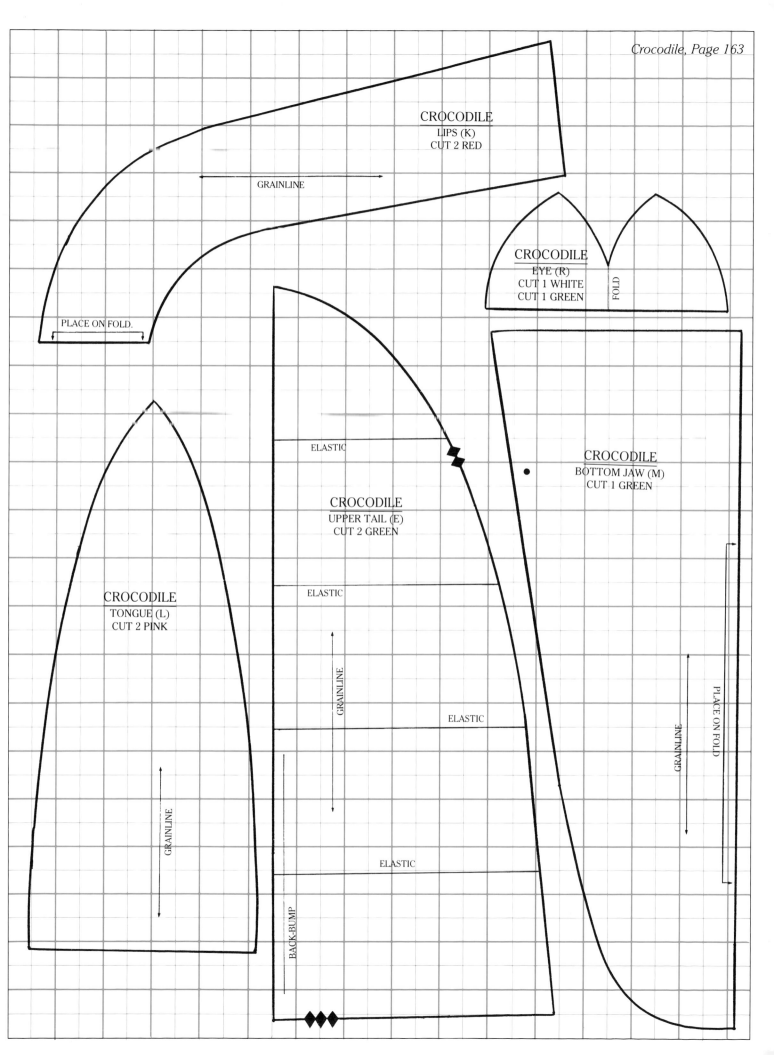

CROCODILE
LIPS (K)
CUT 2 RED

GRAINLINE

PLACE ON FOLD.

CROCODILE
EYE (R)
CUT 1 WHITE
CUT 1 GREEN

FOLD

CROCODILE
BOTTOM JAW (M)
CUT 1 GREEN

ELASTIC

CROCODILE
UPPER TAIL (E)
CUT 2 GREEN

ELASTIC

CROCODILE
TONGUE (L)
CUT 2 PINK

GRAINLINE

PLACE ON FOLD

ELASTIC

GRAINLINE

ELASTIC

GRAINLINE

BACK-BUMP

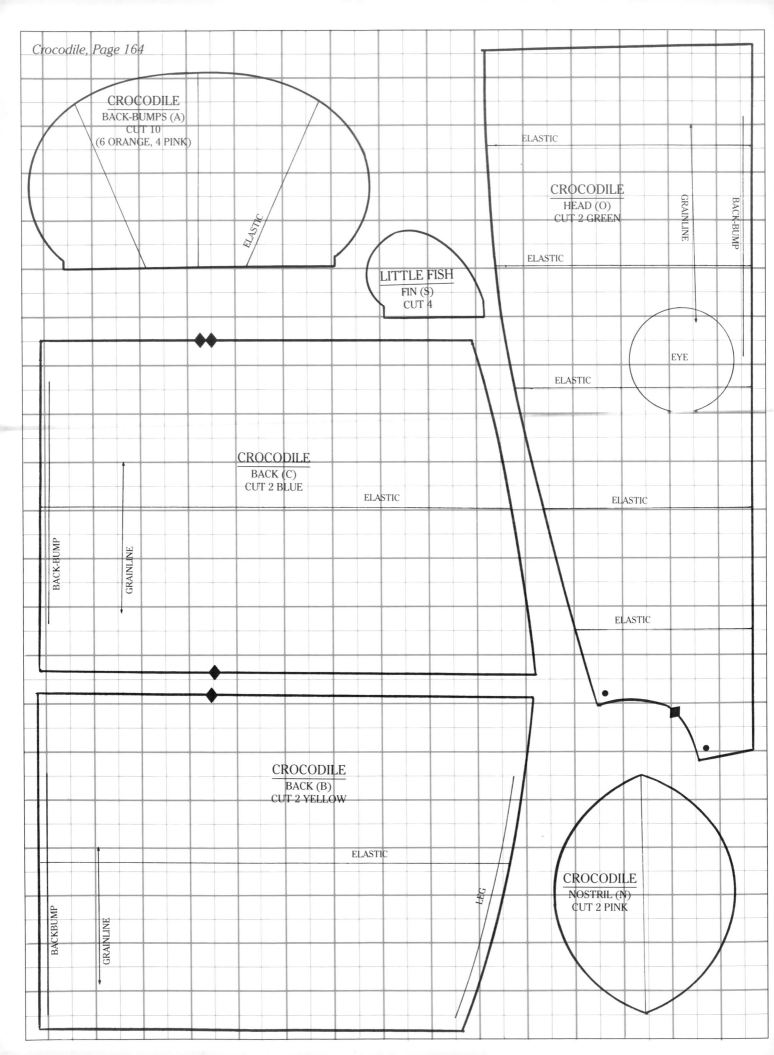

CROCODILE
BACK-BUMPS (A)
CUT 10
(6 ORANGE, 4 PINK)

ELASTIC

CROCODILE
HEAD (O)
CUT 2 GREEN

GRAINLINE

BACK-BUMP

ELASTIC

ELASTIC

LITTLE FISH
FIN (S)
CUT 4

EYE

ELASTIC

CROCODILE
BACK (C)
CUT 2 BLUE

ELASTIC

ELASTIC

BACK-BUMP

GRAINLINE

ELASTIC

CROCODILE
BACK (B)
CUT 2 YELLOW

ELASTIC

LEG

CROCODILE
NOSTRIL (N)
CUT 2 PINK

BACKBUMP

GRAINLINE

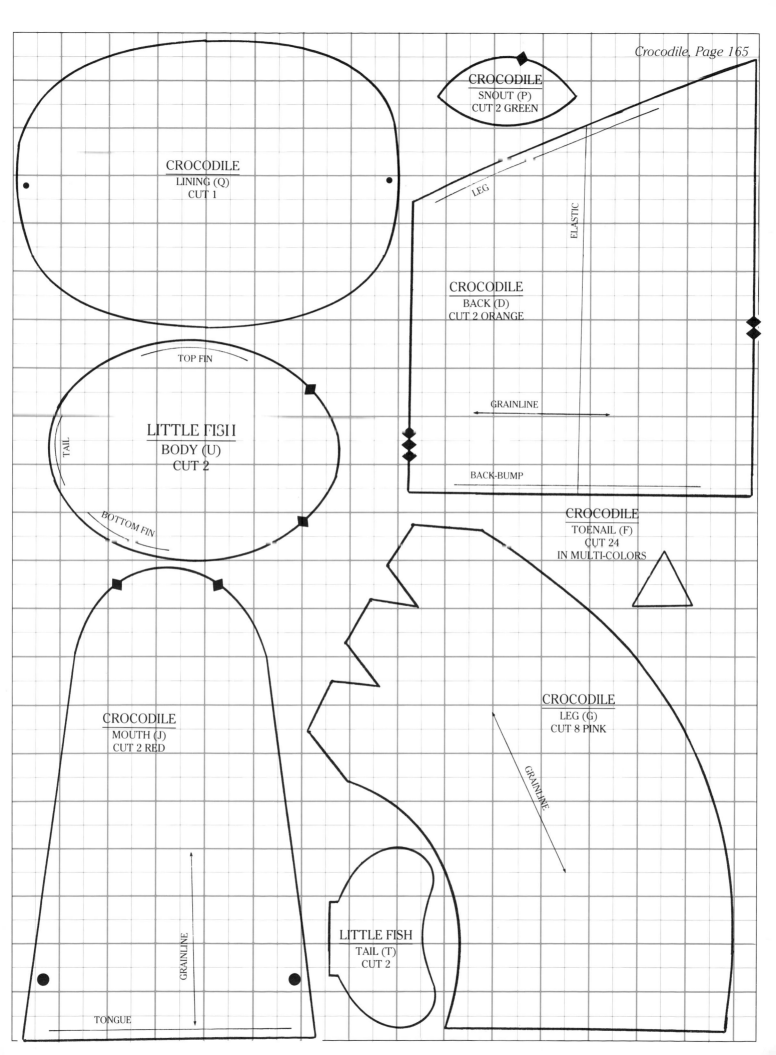

CROCODILE
SNOUT (P)
CUT 2 GREEN

CROCODILE
LINING (Q)
CUT 1

LEG

ELASTIC

CROCODILE
BACK (D)
CUT 2 ORANGE

GRAINLINE

BACK-BUMP

TOP FIN

TAIL

LITTLE FISH
BODY (U)
CUT 2

BOTTOM FIN

CROCODILE
TOENAIL (F)
CUT 24
IN MULTI-COLORS

CROCODILE
MOUTH (J)
CUT 2 RED

CROCODILE
LEG (G)
CUT 8 PINK

GRAINLINE

GRAINLINE

LITTLE FISH
TAIL (T)
CUT 2

TONGUE

GLOSSARY

appendages — Arms and legs or other small body parts attached to main body.

backing — Knit fabric onto which pile of plush fabrics is attached.

baste — To sew with longest possible machine stitches. When hand basting is suggested, hand stitch long running stitches. Use basting as a reinforcing measure, for gathering, ease stitching and pre-stitching seams.

blanket stitch — An embroidery stitch used for overcasting or reinforcing.

clip corner — To create a crisp corner when turned right-side-out. Cut seam allowance from inside corner to pivot in stitching line. Do not cut seam.

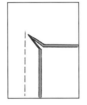

clip curve — To prevent pulling when an inward curve is turned out. Cut seam allowance to seam. Do not cut seam. Repeat so that cuts are evenly spaced along curve.

cutting board — Heavy cardboard which usually folds for storage and comes with a printed grid. Also a plastic board to accompany a cutting wheel.

cutting wheel — Implement for cutting fabrics that looks like a pizza-cutter. Must be used with special cutting board.

dart — Incision in fabric, used for shaping. Position two raw edges, right sides together. Stitch from fold-edge to end.

ease stitch — To decrease length of seam and provide shaping. Baste directly on seam line, then draw up the basting by pulling bobbin thread until seam is the desired length. Check

length by pinning to corresponding pattern piece. Stitch final seam directly on top of ease stitching to prevent puckering.

embroidery thread — Six-strand thread with a satiny texture, used for all forms of embroidery. Can be separated and used in multiple strands of two, three or four.

filling — Material used specifically for stuffing. Synthetic filling is available in three qualities: Fiberfil, the lowest quality; Hollofil, medium range and Qualofil, the highest quality. Fillings are also available under other brand names.

fray — Unravelling which occurs at a raw edge of fabric.

French knots — A simple embroidery stitch, using three or four strands of six-strand embroidery thread.

gather — To create a ruffled texture or shorten a seam. Baste, then pull on one or both ends of the bobbin thread. Adjust gathers for evenness and tie ends off. To keep gathers in place, stay stitch the gathered seam.

grain — In woven fabrics only (not knits), the direction of the thread. To test for grain, pull one thread to form a line.

grid — An intersecting pattern of horizontal and vertical lines that forms squares.

grommet — A flat metal disc with a hole in the center, used to secure commercial plastic eyes.

hand tack — To secure temporarily by hand stitching several stitches in one place, or by long running stitches.

ladder stitch — To sew by hand an invisible seam on right side of fabric. Fold raw

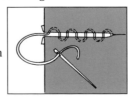

edges to wrong side. Pick up five to six stitches in a running, zigzag fashion from both sides of seam. Draw tightly. When sewing on an animal's head or closing a long area, tie off every so often without breaking the thread, then continue. Repeat to end of seam. Tie off.

lining — Fabric for use inside sewn piece.

markings — Notches, large and small dots and other notations on pattern pieces which aid in aligning sections.

memory — In stretch fabrics and the like, the ability to return to its original size or shape after being stretched.

nap — In plush fabrics, the direction in which the pile lays. Test for nap by running hand in line with the selvedge. The direction of the nap has the *least* resistance. Not all pile fabrics have nap.

notch curve — Prevents bunching when an outward curve is turned right-side-out. Cut V shapes into seam allowance to stitching line, without cutting seam. Cut several V's evenly spaced along curve.

notches — Markings along pattern edge to help in alignment of sections. Cut notches outward or mark on wrong side of fabric.

nylon — A very strong, fast drying, synthetic fiber available in many different weaves. For soft toys, purchase a weave that frays very little.

pile — The soft fuzzy surface fibers of plush, velour or other furry fabrics.

pins — Use extra large or bead-headed pins when sewing soft toys for high visibility and easy retrieval. Never use steel pins as they can become lost in the toy.